God

this is a

good book!

Rich Work

ISBN 0-9648002-1-7

 Asini Publishing
2042 Ryan Rd
Mosinee, WI 54455

Cover Art by
Ali Miner

Printed in the United States by
MISSION POSSIBLE
Commercial Printing
P.O. Box 1495
Sedona, AZ 86339

Dedicated to Ann Marie Groth,
an inspiration and guiding force,
cocreating with me
to bring forth
universal truth
to humanity.

Acknowledgments

I wish to acknowledge all the beautiful souls, seen and unseen, who are bringing forth their gifts to create a positive change, moving our world and our universe from one of limitation, to one where only the divine expression of creative love flourishes.

Poems by Ann Marie Groth

Ann Marie's delightful approach
to awaken consciousness
to the beauty of the world
within and around us
is reflected through her poems.
I thank her for sharing them with us.

Cover Art
"In the Beginning"

by Ali Miner

About the Artist
by Rich Work

As a young boy, I became fascinated with the arts. It began with musical instruments, but quickly turned to drawing and painting. During my early school years, rather than concentrating on my class work, you could often find my attention focused on drawing the girl who sat across the aisle. In later years my interests would shift to another form of art when I became deeply involved in producing movies.

I have watched the changes in art over the years. I stand in awe of the talented artists who are coming forth at this time, giving us new, exciting interpretations with emphasis on colors and expressions never before seen.

As I looked at Ali Miner's beautiful painting "In the Beginning," I knew it had to be a part of this present creation, *God this is a good book!* Each of Ali's magnificent creations of images and writings is a masterpiece of inspiration, made available in her book, *A Time to Awaken.* Her treasures have found their way around the world. For more information regarding her work, contact:

The Consciousness Line,
P.O. Box 491,
Pebble Beach, CA 93953
(408) 641-0845
Fax(408) 641-0349

Foreword

by Ann Marie

As a little girl, I began to see the world through different eyes. Through most of my life I conformed to society and bought many of its belief systems even though deep inside I knew a better way. Confronted with a life-threatening disease, I began to awaken, to discover and live my truth.

Rich Work has spent most of his life following his heart and living his truth. In that journey he discovered that truth continually changes as conscious awareness expands. And it is not the knowing of your truth, but the living of your truth that truly changes your life.

As I heard his many stories, my heart would soar with anticipation as new perceptions and understanding awakened within me.

A potpourri of revelations and insights, this book touches the heart and gently nudges us to remember — to remember who we are and why we are here; to remind us of the divine nature of our being; to express the creative love and desires buried deep within.

I invite you to read this book through the eyes of an innocent child and allow yourself be open to the possibilities.

All I can say is: God this is a good book!

About the Author

Author of *Awaken to the Healer Within*, Rich believes that true healing comes from within. He has worked with thousands in the United States and Canada who have manifested their healing into reality — physically, emotionally, spiritually, financially and socially. From mended souls to mended bodies, the testimonies are too numerous to mention.

For more than thirty years, Rich's path has been one of finding his own answers and empowering others with the tools he has learned.

Rich Work

On the leading edge of understanding the journey of the soul and taking the mystery out of mastery, he demonstrates to us the simplicity of healing and takes us on a beautiful gentle journey of understanding our relationship to the world and those around us.

Having personally conquered cancer, heart disease, mercury poisoning, chronic fatigue syndrome, malaria and asbestos poisoning, his pursuit of the healing arts has brought him to the awareness of the ability to heal from within and bring into harmony the totality of all that we are.

In the business world Rich was an organizer who through necessity had to see the big picture. It was natural that when he was faced with extraordinary health challenges, his mind looked for the broadest perspective from which to view the human healing process. He believes it is time to put an end to making a career out of healing our being and move into the celebration of life.

Conducting lectures and "Awaken to the Healer Within" and "Mastery for Life" workshops, Rich has dedicated his life to bring forth and share those tools and concepts that will assist in expanding the consciousness of mankind and healing the world.

Preface

The writings contained in this book are a reflection of my experiences and conversations with my highest consciousness. These presented themselves to me in the form of dreams, visions, inspirations, revelations, angels, master teachers, guides, the wise one, and similar terms.

We are connected to all consciousness. Your highest self is the totality of your soul and the sum total of every experience your soul has ever had since the beginning of creation. Your soul has many levels of consciousness. Therefore I choose to call forth my highest self. Messages from your highest self never tell you what to do, but empower you to make choices from a broader perspective. They expand your awareness of the world around you, stretching your imagination and giving you new viewpoints to awaken the multitude of possibilities.

As you call forth your knowingness, go within and call forth your highest self and your answers will be genuine and pure.

Contents

Discernment

We are in a universal school where many lessons are being shared, but none are more important than the one of discernment. It is a lesson that will confront you again and again until you have embodied the principle of the lesson, and that is to listen with your heart.

All truth is truth, but not all truth is your truth.

There are many who will try to tell you what your truth is. If you allow them, they will.

It is for you to discern what is right for you. That is the lesson.

As we awaken to our truths, teachers will come forth to see if we will listen with our heart, our intuition, our feelings. The heart connection is the direct connection to universal knowledge.

Your eyes want to believe what they see.
Your ears want to believe what they hear.
Your heart can neither see, nor can it hear.
It knows.
Listen with your heart.

Energy

Energy: The capacity for work or vigorous activity; power. Vitality and intensity of expression. A source of usable power. The capacity of a physical system to do work.

What is energy? Science has long known that everything you can see and perceive is energy. The birds, the bees, the grass, the trees and, yes, you and I are nothing more than energy. Even thoughts and emotions are energy. If all things are energy, then money and time are also. For energy to exist, it must complete an energy cycle. Energy that is created by a generator travels through wires into and through your lights and electrical devices and back through another wire to complete a cycle of energy. This we understand because we have created a solid device that we can see and even draw the principle of it on paper. However, let us use our imagination, for we understand that energy comes from the Creator and goes to all forms of its creation, through them, returning to the Creator to complete the cycle.

The Creator expresses Itself in many forms. We know that you and I are expressions of the Creator, but let us expand this to acknowledge that all life forms upon this planet, including air, clouds, water, mountains, rocks, minerals — the very Earth itself — are expressions of the Creator. Reach out farther and acknowledge that the moon, stars, planets, galaxies and universe and beyond are also an expression, an energy, a life form. Even space, which many believe to be an empty void, is also living energy. Having allowed our consciousness to expand outward, now let it expand inward to the cells, molecules, atoms, particles and other energies within, and know that each is an individual expression of the Creator.

We have already mentioned that thoughts and emotions are energy, as is the very soul itself. Imagine the entire path of the cycle of energy as it comes from the Creator, to and through every aspect of Its creation, interacting with each of these life forms so that It may express Itself, then returning to the Creator. Have you ever given thought that the Creator sends the very energy that provides you life, and that you take this energy, enhance it and take it to another level, then return it to the Creator with greater magnification, thus allowing the Creator to express Itself and grow? Life-force energy comes from the Creator, goes through you into the Earth, returning through you to Source. It is completing the cycle of life.

A similar thing takes place with all of creation; however, if we *are* the Creator, that energy also moves through our creation as part of the energy cycle. "Creator of what?" you might ask. Each individual is a creator, and each one is creating every day, though many have never given it thought. Some create music, others create art, writings, automobiles, furniture, cooking, decorating, gardening — let your imagination expand to understand that your every action and thought through every moment of existence is nothing more or less than one creative experience after another, in which your creative expression (energy) becomes the very life form that sustains it. Yes, even washing the dishes and taking out the garbage are creative experiences. Without creative thought forms, nothing could exist. With this understanding, you may now begin to appreciate the power that you hold within your own creative thought form.

Imagine the sequence that takes place when you turn the radio on. Electricity comes from Source, through the wires and a series of electronic devices that select and amplify a radio frequency that has been resonating in the air around you all the time. The radio decodes these signals, converts them into sound and amplifies them again through the speaker in a form we can hear. Then the electricity returns to Source to complete the cycle of energy — then begins the cycle all over again, because if the cycle stops, the radio stops.

If this is true, what about thought forms? Remember, everything in creation is energy. Every thought you think has a frequency, and frequencies have a vibration. The letter A has a different frequency than B, which has a different frequency than C and so on. Every syllable, word or thought form you invoke has its own set of frequencies that resonate throughout every cell, molecule and atom of the 100 trillion cells in your body, which is known as *your* universe. This includes your energy field, or aura. In other words, it affects your entire being. *Love* has a different frequency than *fear*. When you focus on love, the frequencies of joy, harmony and peace resonate throughout your universe. When you focus on fear, frequencies of anger, depression and chaos are the messages your universe receives.

Your universe translates English, Spanish, French, Swahili or Zulu as a series of frequencies just as your computer does. The universe and computer both respond to frequencies. When you strike a key on your computer keyboard, it records a series of long and short frequencies. This is interpreted and appears on the screen in a form that matches the key you pressed. Therefore

A on the keyboard becomes A on the screen. The computer does not need the A to function — you do. The computer needs only a series of frequencies that it stores in its brain.

Your universe responds in a similar manner. Love (unconditional love) spoken in any language resonates at the highest frequencies in this universe. The concepts and expressions "life-force energy," "universal energy," "light" (universal light) "God" and "love" (unconditional love) all resonate at this same frequency. When you focus on love, that frequency resonates throughout every part of your universe and every cell. Every vibration of your being becomes attuned to that frequency, much like tuning a piano or a guitar will bring it into harmony. When you focus on fear, it instantly creates disharmonic frequencies in your being.

There is a universal law that says
no two things can occupy the same space at the same time.
Light and shadow
never occupy the same space at the same time.
Love and fear
never occupy the same place at the same time.

Can disease occupy a cell wherein God is present?

Let us look at this from a broader perspective. Energy comes to us from Source (the Creator). We take that energy, much like a radio, pass it through our electronic devices — our mind, ego and brain — create thought patterns, amplify them with emotions, voice and actions and send that energy throughout the universe and back to Source. That is correct. I said that *every thought* that you think and every action you take resonates through the universe, affecting everyone around you, your world, your universe and, yes, even your Creator.

If everyone were filled with joy, peace and harmony and in harmony with every other person in the world, what kind of a world would we have?

Science acknowledges that you can neither create nor destroy energy, you can only change its form. As we create something, we never create *more* energy, but rather take energy that already exists and change it into that form which we desire.

Mankind has yet to discover the full potential of the power of the mind, because most of mankind has been focused on the power of limitation, focusing their minds on all the things they cannot do. It is time to let go of old thought patterns and rediscover that all things are possible and that the mind is a powerfully creative tool.

How does a thought form manifest into reality? The human experience is a series of many electrical systems, which we interpret as mind, body and soul functioning together as one reality. Thought forms are also energy that we "create" and send through this maze of electrical systems, which is then sent to a universal consciousness in which all knowledge already exists, and this energy is then returned to manifest our desires. If your electrical systems are dysfunctional, fragmented or distorted, the thought form becomes distorted and thus is sent out and returns distorted. We may see them as dramas and traumas. If your electrical systems are blocked, the thought form may never have the opportunity to be completed.

As we take universal energy (an energy that already exists) and exercise our creative minds, giving that energy meaning and direction with thought, the most powerful energy in the universe, we now have set into motion creative manifestation. Realize that you have been doing this your entire life. Thought is energy set into motion. The spoken or written word is no more than the expression of thought, but never assume that because you refrained from verbalizing it, the thought failed to be set into motion or lacks power.

You may desire to set your intent for all thought forms you embrace.

Intent

From the Divine Love that flows within my Being,
It is my desire to be Well, Whole and Perfect
in Mind, Body and Soul.
It is my intent that all proclamations that I say this day,
and each day,
reflect through all Time and Space and Beyond,
before, between and after Time and Space,
and on all levels of my Being.
I call forth the nucleus of my Being,
the very core of my Wholeness,
to integrate with me in Unconditional Love
in Mind, Body and Spirit to accept this Healing.
So be it.

Many would agree that it is possible to communicate telepathically. Some might agree that a few people can even do it. I suggest that you have done it all your life without being conscious of it. I also find it interesting that people refer to animals as dumb because they are unable to talk, drive a car, make mortgage payments or fill out tax papers. Yet animals are far more advanced in communication skills than we are, since all species communicate telepathically, something we have forgotten that we are capable of. Animals must find it amusing that humans feel they must move their lips and make noises to be understood, and that some humans believe the louder the noise, the more likely they will be heard. Dogs, cats and horses understand your thoughts and read your emotions far better than most give them credit for.

When communicating telepathically with another person, there is no necessity to know where they are, any more than it is for you to know where the person is whose cellular phone you dial. The message goes directly to the person you hold in your intent, because that person is the only one who holds that vibration. If you are lost in the woods, you may be able to communicate telepathically with someone, but if you want someone to locate you, you shout "help!" to give them direction.

How do thought and telepathic ability apply to us? Telepathic communication is the natural form of communication and yes, you probably have already done it. Have you prayed silently for someone? "God Bless Mommy and Daddy and all my angels"? Was your prayer heard? You believed your prayer would be heard or you would never have said it.

Was this a telepathic message? In telepathic communication, the question is, is the receiver of this message turned on, open to receive the message, or does he have his walls up and the receiver shut down? The day is rapidly approaching when tele-pathic communication will be quite common, as we will begin to remember this ability we have always had, one without a lan-guage barrier, one that allows us to communicate with all mankind as well as animals and all life forms, each having a cre-ative consciousness.

Thought is a powerful tool. Many creative expressions appear to be undesirable. You may see war as undesirable for many people, but it is nevertheless a creative expression. Some desire this creative expression because it gives them purpose and power, yet for others it brings fear, judgment, destruction and pain. This creative expression will continue to exist until it is changed or transmuted into another creative expression, preferably one that will bring joy to all.

Now, let's put it all together in a simple demonstration. In our world we have been subjected to all forms of toxic metals and residues. They come from our polluted water, air and soil. They come from our food, laundry detergents, medicines (many pre-scription drugs contain toxic metals and chemicals), radiation from our environment, electromagnetic diagnostic equipment and many other distorted energies we come in contact with. Most people feel defenseless against such an onslaught of ener-gies that are negative to the human experience, yet all of us have within our being the ability to transmute these toxins into an energy that will serve us. This ability lies within the mind and the power of thought. You are a great alchemist, and it is time that you awaken to the true master that you are. The following is an affirmation that will allow you to accomplish all of which we speak.

Transmuting Toxic Metals and Toxic Residues

From the Divine Love that flows within my Being,
allow now that my Divine Light,
my Light of Love,
my Light of Healing,
my Light of Protection,
my Light of Power and Wisdom,
become a permanent part of every molecule
of the toxic metals in my body
now and throughout my lifetime.
I include all toxic residues
on all levels of my Being,
through all Time and Space and Beyond
and between Time and Space.
Allow that they resonate
at the highest frequency of Unconditional Love.
And no one shall change this proclamation
until I do so of my own Free-Will Choice.
So be it.

Did this really happen? What was your intent? Remember, the Master said, "Ask and you shall receive." He never said, "Ask and we'll have a committee meeting and take a vote on it."

These energies will no longer deplete your energy, but enhance it. Why? Because you have taken these low vibrational frequencies that create stress in your being and transmute them into the higher frequencies of unconditional love.

Is it possible that you transmuted toxic residues? During the introduction to one of our workshops, I demonstrated on a volunteer how to transmute those things mentioned above. The next morning a lady in the workshop was absentmindedly running her fingers through her long black hair. What I was unaware of is that she had breast cancer and was on heavy doses of chemotherapy. Of course, one of the side effects is that your hair tends to fall out. Running her fingers through her hair through habit, she would then reach down to brush the loose hair from her dress. When she realized there was no hair on her dress, she deliberately ran her fingers through her hair again and found that it was no longer falling out. She was so excited that she stopped me in the middle of a sentence to tell me what she had discovered. She asked, "What's going on?"

I said, "You were at the introduction last night when I demonstrated transmuting toxic metals and residues. When I performed that demonstration, you repeated and embodied the affirmation I offered as your own, is that so?"

"Yes" she replied.

"You have your validation," I stated. "You transmuted the toxic side effects of your chemotherapy."

Some have told me, "I have said affirmations before, but they have done little to change in my life." It is important to understand that lip service fails to get the job done. For a thought form to manifest, it must complete a cycle of energy. If you maintain old belief patterns at any level of consciousness, it creates a blockage or distortion that interferes with the free flow of energy. To say, "I would like to jump across the ditch" while maintaining a belief that you are unable to jump across it, means that you will be unable to do so. You may call forth your prosperity, but if you feel unworthy of being prosperous, you have cut off the flow of energy. If you affirm that you no longer wish to have your disease, yet harbor a feeling that you are sick and tired of life, the ultimate outcome should be obvious.

There is no frequency in negative thought.
To focus on a negative thought stops the flow of energy,
like turning off the switch.

Your subconscious mind has no sense of humor. It is there to serve you and will respond to your every thought. Each thought form has its own frequency. Negative thought has none. Doubt and indecision are negative thoughts or energies. When doubt and indecision enter, nothing moves. It is like holding your breath. When you hold your breath, the *Breath of Life* is absent. "Cancer" is not a negative thought. Cancer is a distorted energy. Cancer is a disharmonic energy. Cancer may be undesirable, but it is not negative. Cancer is a powerful frequency. Cancer is the manifestation of suppressed anger. It is time to reevaluate the thoughts we think and the words we choose.

What would you do if you suddenly became aware that you have set into motion an undesirable thought such as "I'm just *dying* to get a new car?" Simply state, "I rescind that thought," and create one that is more desirable.

There is yet another way to assure that thoughts out of alignment with your highest consciousness will have no effect, and that is to *reprogram* your computer — your mind. Have you ever tried to put something into a computer that the computer was never programmed to accept? It will reject it — and so it is with your mind computer. After all, *you* are the alchemist. You are divine love expressed.

Aligning My Highest Consciousness

All proclamations that I say this day and each day,
I will accept only those
that are in alignment with my Highest Consciousness.
So be it.

✧ ✧ ✧ ✧

It is time to expand your consciousness — to creatively manifest whatever will bring your world into one of joy. In doing so, remember always to honor the free-will choice of another.

There is no ultimate human experience.

When the soul grows, all aspects of you grow, and there is no "ultimate" human experience. To smell a rose, to taste sweet nectar, to hear the sound of music and to feel the peace and contentment of your heart are only a few of many great human experiences. Think back to the time of the creation of the Earth and why it was created — then to your own human experiences through thousands of life experiences. What was the greatest experience you have had in any aspect of your being?

I believe you will discover the answer is, the birth of your creative energy and the manifestation of its form, delighting the essence of the soul. Is there anything more grand than seeing Divine Love in action in creative manifestation? It is the greatest experience any being can ever have in any universe.

Universal Laws

There are universal laws that govern us regardless of whether we are aware of them. These are the laws by which we create and manifest our reality.

1. The Law of Magnetic Attraction

You attract to you that which you desire. You also attract that which you find undesirable — if you focus on it. If you focus on disease, you will manifest more disease. If you focus on poverty, you will manifest more poverty. If you focus on the lack of love in your life, you will manifest only more lack. It is impossible to create love when you focus on fear. It is impossible to create prosperity when you focus on poverty. It is the law of magnetic attraction.

2. The Law of Creative Manifestation

Now that you understand law number one, invoke law number two. Intentionally focus on that which you desire; avoid focusing on that which you find undesirable in your life. If you are in a room where others are engaged in a conversation about something you find undesirable in your life, politely excuse yourself and leave. To remain in that energy will only attract more of it into your life.

3. The Law of Allowing

The most difficult law of all. Put your thoughts into universal consciousness reinforced by desire. Then step aside and allow the universe to manifest it for you. If you are hoping, you are not allowing. If you have expectations, you are not allowing. The more you expect, the more you hope, the more you try to manage or control, then the more you will interfere with and retard the manifesting of your desires. The law of "allowing" means just that.

Remember, everything in creation is energy. Every thought you think has a frequency. Every syllable, word or thought form you invoke has its own set of frequencies that resonate throughout your universe.

When you focus on love,
frequencies of joy, harmony and peace
resonate throughout your universe.
When you focus on fear,
frequencies of anger, depression and chaos
are the messages your universe receives.

Messages

by Ann Marie

All knowledge and wisdom lie within.
It is but a moment from your awareness.
Taking the time to focus your thoughts
opens the doorways you desire.

Dedicating a few moments each day
to go within — and listen,
expanding reality to all the possibilities
is the greatest investment of all time.

Gathering the seeds of wisdom from within,
enter your heart center with pen in hand.
As you relax into the peace and feel the smile within,
begin to write that which comes forth.
Be it a color, a sound or a phrase,
write down that which you perceive.

Have no expectations.
The more often you ask, the more you receive.
You are learning to go within.
More important,
you are learning to listen.

My Truth

I stood upon a hill one night
looking for my truth.
Where is this universe about which I have so often heard?
Is it true there is more than my eyes can see?
I strained to see into the darkness
to view the twinkling stars.
Is there more? I asked,
and saw a meteor streaking through the night.
There must be many mysteries, I thought,
that lie beyond my sight.

And as I stood throughout the long hours
the night gave way to light.
First the darkness turned to gray,
then light would crest the horizon.
Perhaps the answers I sought will come with the rising sun.
I waited patiently. The sun appeared,
and now I could see the beautiful clouds
and the land that surrounded me,
but with the rising sun
I could no longer see the twinkling stars.

As I stood,
I realized that I had seen only a token
of what the universe has to offer,
but where else could I go to find it?

Disappointed
and only partially rewarded for my efforts,
I returned to my home and entered.
I found myself standing before my looking glass.
I paused, for suddenly I realized
I had found that which I was seeking.
For the first time I could see the Earth in its entirety . . .
the universe, the galaxy, even Creation itself.
Chills ran through me as I became aware
that I had looked into this mirror every day
but had never seen that which I had longed for.
Standing before me in my mirror
was the totality of Divine Love expressed.
The universe that I had sought so long to see
was within me.

I rushed out the door
to announce my discovery to the world,
but once outside I stopped short
as I saw the beautiful flowers.
I paused to kneel before them
and smell their fragrance as never before,
only to realize that they too were Divine Love expressed.

Slowly I looked around,
my eyes capturing the panorama that surrounded me . . .
the green grass, the magnificent trees,
the colorful birds, the bees busily at work,
the butterflies caressing everything they touched.

I heard a door open, then close.
I looked up to see my neighbors on their porch.
I looked again,
for today I saw them through different eyes.
They too were Divine Love expressed.
I realized that Creation itself
has been created in everything my eyes could see
or that my mind could perceive.

Again I returned to stand before my mirror.
I stood in awe as I looked upon my universe,
my truth, the miracle of life,
Divine Love expressed.

My Special Day

Here I sit under the old oak tree, my fishing pole in my hand and the quiet brook just beyond my feet. It is so peaceful as I watch the bobber on my line. I come here often — to sit, to fish, to reflect upon my life. The bobber bounces once in the water and stops. Was it a fish, or did I bump my pole? It doesn't matter. I have lots of time, for today is my special day. Today is my birthday and I can take as long as I want.

The blue sky peeks between the clouds, a butterfly lands on the end of my pole as if to say, "Hello, I have come to greet you on your special day."

My mind wanders. Life seems so confusing — so many things to choose from, so many things to do, so many things to learn, so much work to be done. But that can wait, for this is my special day: today is my birthday.

A squirrel scampers down the tree. I sit very still. It stops, looks toward me, stands on its hind legs and chatters to see if I'm real or if I am just another part of the playground it lives in. It watches for a movement. The perky ears, the silky fur coat, the tail twitching with excitement. It seems to express every part of its being with every movement it makes, as if each moment is meant to express and live everything it is. There appears to be no concern about what it did a moment ago or what it will do in the future. It lives for the moment it is in.

In one last effort to test me it runs up my leg, jumps up and down, sits, chatters a greeting to me and hurries off into the woods to find something for breakfast.

Something catches my eye and I shift my gaze to the ground to see a caterpillar moving slowly on its journey. What a funny-looking creature — but then it must think I look funny, too. It has many legs and moves so slowly. Its world is so big, yet small compared to mine. I have so many teachers, I thought.

My bobber disappeared under the water, and with great excitement I pulled up on my pole. The line came easily, with nothing to show but an empty hook. I reached into my tin can and took out another worm, blessed it and carefully placed it on the hook, just like my father had taught me. He had taught me so many things, but it was my mother who had taught me to tie my shoes.

I turned and carefully swung my pole so that my bobber and hook would reach that special spot where I knew I would catch my fish. I rested against the big oak tree again, wondering how old it was and how many others had sat there under its cool shade to use my fishing hole.

Something moved in the water — it was a frog. My fishing hole was always alive with activity. You could always find tadpoles, and sometimes I saw a turtle. My most special day was when a deer and its baby came to drink. They stood for a long time just across the brook from me, first looking at me with their big brown eyes as if to say, "We live here too, and we are glad to share our home with you." Then they drank some water and finally moved off into the woods.

Again the bobber moved, only slightly, then there were three big jerks. Excitement ran through me as I pulled up on my pole.

The water swirled as a big fish came bursting out of the water. I pulled so hard that the fish went right over my head and landed on the ground behind me. I carefully removed it from the hook and held it before me. It was probably the biggest fish I had ever caught. As I looked at it, it said, "I have come today to grace your table and provide food for you and your family — for this is your special day."

Excitedly I placed my beautiful fish in the bucket I had brought and added some water. I picked up my pole and my can of worms — as well as the peanut butter and jelly sandwich I hadn't taken time to eat. As I turned to begin my journey to my house and my family, I thought, This is truly an exciting day for me, for this is my special day. Today is my birthday. Today I am six years old.

Who Are You?

by Ann Marie

Who am I?
Where did I come from?
Why am I here?
are questions so often asked.

Birthed in the heart of the Creator
you are a divine expression of creative love.
You came to experience separation
in a world of limitation and fear,
getting lost in illusion . . . forgetting your identity,
playing a game you forgot how to end.

But now you choose to remember,
to remember who you are,
to live a life of joy,
peace and harmony,
the life your heart already knows.
A divine being of creative love
waiting to be expressed,
to put into practice
that which has been learned.

*To express worry and fear
creates frustration.
To express frustration and anxiety
creates disharmony.
To express limitation and hoarding
creates luck.
To express judgment, anger and insecurity
creates distress.*

*To express fulfillment and desire
creates joy.
To express contentment and joy
creates peace.
To express patience and trust
creates harmony.
To express awareness and appreciation
creates miracles.
To express the beauty from within
creates the celebration of life.*

*You are an expression of Love
You came from the Source of Love
You came to express that Love . . .*

*You truly become that which you express.
You are the creator of your world.
What reality do you choose?*

We

We have a lot in common, you and I.
We sometimes agree
and sometimes we disagree,
but nevertheless we still have a lot to share.
We may have different-colored skin
and we may have different beliefs,
but we still have a lot in common, you and I.

We might disagree on how to raise our children
or where they should go for their education
or even what education they should receive.
We might come from different social classes
and have different spiritual beliefs,
but we have a lot in common, you and I.

We may differ on political issues
and we might choose to live in different parts of the world.
We might not always agree on what foods are best
and have different opinions
on how to address our health issues,
but we have a lot in common, you and I.

We might disagree on what colors
to decorate our homes or to adorn our bodies
or on the style of furniture or clothes we prefer.
We might differ on music, dance or creative art,
but we will always have a lot in common, you and I.

What do we have in common
that makes our relationship so unique?
It is that we all have free-will choice.
Each one has been created and endowed
with one law from Creator Source —
the law of free-will choice.

You are free to explore,
to create and to experience those creations.
You might go left, you might go right,
you can go up or down.
You might bang your head against the wall
to find it brings you pain,
or choose to play and find it brings you joy.
The choices are many; we have mentioned only a few.

We can choose from a variety of music,
dance, art and social issues —
the list is endless.
And each day brings a new experience
from which we can make a choice.

The universal law of free-will choice has only one limitation:
You may exercise your free-will choice
as long as you refrain from violating
the free-will choice of another.
To exercise your free-will choice
is to live your truth.
To allow others to exercise their free-will choice
is to allow them to live their truth.
To do so is to honor all others.
To do so is to stand in unconditional love.
To do so is to be in a state of being without judgment —
of yourself or of others.
To do so is to honor all persons
for the journey they have chosen
and the choices they have made,
even though they differ from yours.
We were never intended to be clones of one another,
but to experience all that creation offers.
It is how the soul grows.

Regardless of our color,
our beliefs or our differences
we still have a lot in common, you and I.
We come from the same Creator Source —
the same cosmic play dough from which all things are made.
We have only chosen a different journey
that we may experience the totality of All That Is.

We have a lot in common, you and I.

The Nature of Things

by Ann Marie

To know the love of another . . .
you must first find it within yourself.
You manifest
only that which reflects from your heart.

Your heart is the center of your world.
Your world is the reflection of your heart.
That is the nature of things.

Like an adventurer
in quest of buried treasure,
prepare to take a gentle journey
into the realms within
to find the precious gem of love
just waiting to be found.

Close your eyes . . .
let your mind be still.
Begin to drift
on the waves of your breath.

Imagine:
a radiant light . . .
the divine essence of love
deep within.

Drifting deeper into the radiance,
imagine yourself becoming tiny,
very tiny . . .
tinier than your heart,
and let yourself be
completely
immersed in the radiance of love.

With each breath
breathe in the radiance
and feel your body
filling
with shimmering waves of golden light.

Embraced in the waves of light,
perceive the gentle touch
caressing every aspect of
your being.

You are now inside your heart center
totally surrounded
and filled
with radiant love.

You came looking for treasure
and found the ocean of love.
You had looked for it outside . . .
and found it dwelling within.

I m a g i n e
c o m p l e t e l y
f i l l i n g
y o u r   b e i n g
w i t h   r a d i a n t   l o v e .

Abundant streams of radiance
flow in and around your being,
from your heart into the reality of your world.

Let your dreams and visions
come to mind,
floating out on the waves of love
to carry forth your call for love,
to be answered by the call for love in another.

Now that you have found the love within yourself
you can find it in another.
The reflection of your love
allows another to see it in you.
That is the nature of things.

36 ✧ GOD THIS IS A GOOD BOOK!

Mother Earth

I sat in my favorite chair and reflected on the message I had received from my friend. I laid the letter on my lap, closed my eyes and tried to visualize what its contents implied.

> "We are asking everyone to focus their intent, collectively, at a specific time, using meditation and prayer for the purpose of healing the Earth . . ."

Something troubled me. The longer I thought about the message, the more I felt something was incomplete.

"How can I assist you?" my highest consciousness asked.

"Hello," I replied, "I was just about to call on you. How did you know?"

"When your thoughts turn to me, I am instantly in communication with you. After all, I am your highest consciousness. I am aware of the message that you have received. How can I assist you?"

"There is something in this message that troubles me, and I can't determine what it is."

"Why don't you repeat the message one more time?"

I raised the letter from my lap and read aloud. *"We are asking everyone to focus their intent, collectively, at a specific time, using meditation and prayer for the purpose of healing the Earth . . ."*

"Something is missing. What have I failed to see?" I asked.

"What is it you are being asked to do?"

"I am being asked to heal the Earth."

"Who has asked you to heal the Earth?"

"My friend," I said. "He wants me to join in a collective effort to heal the Earth."

"Has the Earth asked you for a healing?"

"No. How could the Earth ask me for a healing?"

"The Earth is a living entity with a consciousness, no less than you are. If the Earth was asking for a healing, your intuitive self would know it instantly. There would be no doubt in your mind."

"Yes, I know that is true," I said. "If you listen with your heart, you will know. I guess that's what is bothering me. The language used implies fixing the Earth."

"That is correct. Why would you want to heal someone if no request has been made for your assistance in their healing? How would you like to have a million people standing around you with an intent to fix what they perceive as wrong in you?"

"I wouldn't like it at all," I replied. "Why would anyone want to do that?"

"Because they perceive there is something wrong with the Earth and they would like to *fix* it. Before you would want to fix something, you must first judge it to be imperfect. To judge something is to overlook the divine perfection within it.

"I acknowledge and honor those who have given an effort to help Mother Earth in her healing. While it is a popular thing to do, caution must prevail. It is impossible for you to heal anyone or anything, including Mother Earth. You can only heal yourself — and in so doing, you shift mass consciousness, and in this manner the Earth, the Universe and Creation itself heals.

The Earth is a reflection of humanity.
Disruptions upon the Earth
are the symptoms reflecting disharmony within
individual people upon the Earth.

"Imagine for a moment that your country was at war. Would you first choose to rebuild the country — or would you choose to negotiate peace?"

"I would negotiate peace," I replied. "It makes no sense to rebuild a country that is still being destroyed."

"This is true. When you try to fix something, you are trying to rebuild the country before you have negotiated peace. As each person becomes filled with peace, the Earth will be healed.

"Your societies have spent much of their time trying to heal the symptom rather than eliminate the cause. However, there are ways to accomplish the goals that your friend desires.

Assisting Others in Their Healing

"Many people have reached out to *assist* another in their healing. There are others who have reached out to *fix* others. After all, if we could just fix *them*, then *our* world would be better. Governments and societies have taught us well. If there is something we perceive as wrong, let's fix it. Remember, however, there may be others who want to fix *you*.

"I would never suggest that you refrain from reaching out to others. I am suggesting that there is a difference between assisting and fixing."

Fixing: To fix is to violate the free-will choice of another. It is forcing your energies upon them without permission, regardless of the intent.

Assisting: Assisting is to offer your service — once you have received their permission. However, you may assist only within the boundaries they have set. To do otherwise is to violate their free-will choice.

"Do you recall any situations in your lifetime that would demonstrate the concept of fixing versus assisting?"

"Yes, now that I think about it, I can think of many. Let me share a couple with you," I said.

A young lady asked me to assist her in her healing. She had many problems, and she responded quickly to the healing. At one point I noticed that she had scoliosis (curvature of the spine). I asked if she was aware of this condition. She said she was unaware of it. I quickly added, "Well, I'll take care of that." I energetically worked with her and you could visibly see the spine move into alignment.

A week later I met her again. She acknowledged the profound healing that she had received, then added that her spine had quickly gone out of alignment again. She stated, "I was aware that with each step of the healing you asked my permission, and I gave it to you. However, when you came to my spine, you said, "Well, I'll take care of that." You denied me the opportunity to give my permission, and a permanent healing failed to occur."

This young lady came as my teacher to remind me once again of the importance of never assuming that because you have permission to assist in one area, you have permission in all areas.

I thanked her for being my teacher.

A gentleman was having difficulty with the circulation in his leg, and it caused him great pain. He went to the hospital to find what his options were. They administered general anesthesia before doing exploratory procedures. When he awoke, he found that they had removed his leg. He was furious. He had been violated. They failed to acknowledge his responsibility to be a part of making the decisions in his healing. Often patients have awakened to hear the doctor say, "While we had you open we decided to remove these other parts of your body," even though no permission had been given.

"The stories you have shared occur every day in your world, and those involved would argue that they had good intent. However, it is time to become aware of how your world works and how to focus your creative efforts for the benefit of all.

"Often the person you desire to assist is unavailable to ask. An infant, someone in a coma, or someone who is elsewhere in the moment. *This also applies to the Earth.* She still has free-will choice.

"There is a way in which you may assist all of them if that is your desire. If the person is available, ask for permission. If the person is unavailable, you may call that person forth in spirit with this intent:

I call forth (name) to stand before me,
as I stand before you, in Love.
On your behalf
I offer you this healing to accept or reject
according to your Free-Will Choice.

"Go into your quiet space and silently (or aloud) say your prayers or proclamations on the person's behalf. Avoid becoming attached to the results. You are not responsible for the healing. To have expectations interferes with the natural flow of energy and you may inhibit the very healing you desire to assist. Offer your assistance, then get out of the way. The person will accept that part of the healing for which he or she is prepared to receive.

"With this understanding, you may choose to embrace the following proclamation with the intent of assisting humanity and the Earth in returning it to its most perfected state of being."

I call forth all Souls, the Earth, the elementals,
thought forms and energies to stand before me,
as I stand before you, in Love.
On your behalf
and on behalf of myself,
I offer you this healing to accept or reject
according to your Free-Will Choice.

Almighty indwelling God,
I command you to heal,
instantly and completely.
It is the right of God to heal.
So be it.

✧ ✧ ✧ ✧

"There is another proclamation you might wish to consider," my highest self continued, "as you explore opportunities to cocreate in restoring your universe to its divine essence.

Earth Changes

I give myself permission to assist Mother Earth
in creating energy shifts
that are bringing forth those changes
that bring her and her children peace and joy.
I command that all energies I give forth,
receive or transmute in this effort
be embraced into Unconditional Love
and sent back to their origin
so that they might be used to strengthen
and cocreate with our World in its Divine Perfection.
So be it.

My Friend

As I stood looking down at you, my friend,
I could see the troubled look upon your face
and sense the thoughts that raced through your mind.

Why had life been so cruel, you wondered,
to have treated me this way?
I had always been so active,
busily engaged with the many things life had to offer.
My work, my family, my friends,
so many things to do, so many things to choose from.
There never seemed to be enough time
to complete all that demanded my attention.
Life was so full,
life was so rewarding.
I had accomplished things that others only dream of,
but now my life seems to have come to an end,
for fate has dealt me a crushing blow.
Why, I asked, do I now find myself confined,
unable to move about,
to express myself as I once did?

And as I asked the question
a silent voice whispered in my ear,
"My friend, you have only just begun
to understand and express yourself.

You have spent your life
experiencing your reality through your body,
and now you have been told
it is time to slow down,
to stop and reflect upon your life experience
and to explore another part of your universe —
your mind.

"True expression, true creativity,
are put into action with the mind.
Worlds have been created and worlds have been destroyed
with the power of the mind.
The mind is a part of your soul.

"Your soul is who you are.
Your body is only a vehicle that the soul occupies
to experience in this dimension called Earth.
You have been blessed
with the opportunity to slow down
and reflect upon the blessings
you have received within this lifetime,
what lessons you have learned,
and how you have grown.

"Now is the time to explore your mind.
The mind knows no limitation
other than that which you have placed upon it.

Life never ends; life is eternal.
You are simply completing one chapter
and now find yourself about to open a new one.
Allow it to unfold and discover the love, the peace
and the divine expression that lies within you
and those around you.

"And who am I, you ask,
Who has whispered this message in your ear?
I am your guardian angel.
I have been with you since your birth.
I have been your constant companion,
watching you stumble,
assisting you when you have asked for my help,
watching you grow.
I have never left your side.
I am with you in love.
Although you have never seen me with your physical eyes,
You have felt my presence many times,
and now
as you prepare to leave,
you have only to call me forth,
and when you least expect it
I shall appear before your eyes, my friend."

by Ann Marie

The Universe moves
with the laughter of the heart.
Doorways open
and new realities are seen.

Insights burst forth
to be acknowledged
and magical moments appear . . .
creating more laughter
moving the universe
in the direction of the desires
within your heart

To open the doorways
you need only to use the key.

My Garden of Eden

My tablet rests upon my lap,
my pen rests steadily in my hand,
my mind dwells upon the impossible,
but my heart knows the truth.

My conscious mind reaches into the universe
for the great wisdom,
only to recognize that it lies within.
My mind struggles with the teachings
that have come through the generations,
not wanting to believe they could have been misconceived.
But alas, the mind humbly bows
before the great truths of the universe
as it feels the reassuring resonance
that emanates from universal love,
from universal truth;
to discover that it is I who makes my own truth,
my reality,
to discover that all things are possible
. . . limited only by my beliefs;
to realize that I need only call forth my desires in joy
and allow them to manifest according to universal law
and recognize the gift as it comes forth.

I rescind all thought patterns that I have owned
through all levels of consciousness
that would limit myself from manifesting
according to my heart's desire.

And now I take my pen
and write upon my tablet
my list of all that I desire to manifest in my life:
that which I desire to become my reality,
that which will shape my world once again
into my Garden of Eden,
that which will bring me Joy
according to my heart's desire.

The Angels Are All Around You

by Ann Marie

Angels are all around you,
encouraging you along your way,
sending gentle messages . . . in many special ways.

In your busy life
messages often brushed aside
as nonsense or circumstance
are your intuition . . .
Love the guidance as it comes,
see where it will go.

The seemingly magical moments
are those created
when you are without a care.

Often your doubt will stop them.
Innocent joy
allows them to occur.

Watch the world
with eyes of delight;
it is here you will see the Angels play
assisting you on your way.

The more you acknowledge your Angels
the more their presence will be shown.

Reach out to them,
brush your doubt and fear aside . . .
allow the magic to begin.

The Dental Appointment

"**I** would like to talk to an angel, please," I demanded, speaking out loud.

"I am an angel."

I was startled by the immediate response. "That was fast," I said. "Where were you when I called?"

"Right here. I am with you all the time."

"You are?" I said, surprised. "Who are you?"

"I am your guardian angel," it replied.

"Well, why haven't you talked to me before to let me know you were here?"

"That is not my responsibility," my guardian angel said. "I am here to assist you when you ask for assistance. It is your responsibility to become aware and recognize my presence."

"Well, I sure could have used your help the other day when I needed a parking place at the shopping mall," I said gruffly.

"You need only to ask," the guardian angel responded. "We have angels that some refer to as their 'parking angel.' It is their specialty to arrange a parking space. But you must ask — ask *before* you arrive. Even parking angels require a little time to make those arrangements. Try it sometime as you leave for your destination. Ask the parking angel to prepare space for you. You might be surprised at the results."

"I think I will," I said. "Can you tell me how many angels I have?"

"How many do you want? You already have many who work

with you — and you may call forth any number you wish depending on your desires at the time. We look forward to hearing from you. Remember, there is nothing more restless than a bored angel."

"If you are my guardian angel, that must mean you are supposed to protect me. Where were you last week when I was in heavy traffic and ran into that automobile in front of me? I caused a lot of damage to my car — and someone could have been hurt! Where were you then?"

"I rather enjoyed watching that," said my guardian angel with amusement.

"What?" I exclaimed. "You *enjoyed* seeing me crash my automobile? Do you realize the expense that it caused me, the downtime of having my car repaired, including missing an appointment with my dentist? Do you have any idea how long it takes to get an appointment with a dentist?"

"Yes," the guardian angel replied. "I enjoy watching you create and act out your dramas. It is much like when you go to the movies or a play and watch the drama unfold. In your case I have a front-row seat. I am not here to prevent you from creating your dramas. That is what you have come to experience. I am here to assist you, to offer you direction in your choices — but when and only when you ask for assistance. I would never interfere with your journey. You are participating in the game of life, a game with free-will choice."

"Well, I can tell you, I didn't like the game when I crashed my automobile," I said.

"Then change the rules," said the angel. "Exercise your free-will choice. If crashing your automobile fails to bring you joy, invoke your free-will choice and call forth into your life something that will. That is what we call reclaiming your mastery."

"You said that you would help me if I asked you for help."

"I will assist you," said the angel. "I will assist you by making you aware of your choices — the options available to you according to where you are in the moment and where you desire to go. *You* make the rules in your game of life; you make your own choices. For each situation there are no fewer than three choices. You can take the high road, the middle road or the low road — the easy path, the more difficult path or the most difficult path. Any of them will get you to your destination. And I would remind you that refusing to make a choice is also a choice. It is often the choice that allows others to exercise their free-will choice over you. I have assisted you many times with your choices, although you might have been unaware of it. They were those times when a thought raced through your mind — 'What do I do now?' — and suddenly choices flashed into your mind. Where do you believe they came from?"

"But where were you when I crashed my automobile?" I persisted. "Someone could have been seriously hurt."

"I was with you," replied my angel. "I was there to make sure that no one was injured. After all, you had no intention of injuring anyone else, let alone yourself."

"My intention?" I was exasperated. "What do you mean, my intention? It was that idiot in front of me. If he hadn't hit his brakes, none of this would have happened."

I could hardly believe my ears. My guardian angel was *laughing!* I had never heard an angel laugh before. "Why are you laughing? We're talking serious stuff here," I said, a little miffed.

The laughter became louder. I could hear a whole chorus of angels laughing! I had an audience. "Let's get serious," I said. "I fail to see the humor in all this."

Finally the laughter subsided and my guardian angel regained its composure and said, "Master, what was the last thought that went through your mind just before the accident — if that's what you choose to call it?"

I thought hard. What in the world had I been thinking about? I was on my way to the dentist, I thought. "That's it," I said aloud. "That's it. I was on the way to my dentist to have some molars extracted. All I could think about was the pain I would have to go through. I dislike dentists. It has nothing to do with them — I think they're good people. In fact, one of my best friends is a dentist, but visiting one is my least favorite pastime. I remember now. My last thought was, 'I would give anything if I didn't have to go to the dentist today!'"

"Well?" questioned the angel.

"Well what?"

"Can you see that it was you who created your reality? That this beautiful soul — the one you call an idiot — cocreated your drama with you, stepping on his brakes and providing you the opportunity to miss your dental appointment?"

I was stunned. "You've got to be kidding. You mean that I created all that?"

"Yes, master," replied my guardian angel, "and everything else in your life, although you have often chosen to see yourself as the victim. You have *never* been the victim. You only chose to play victim so you could blame someone or something else for your own manifestation. Thought is the most powerful energy in the universe. Be careful what you ask for — you are the master."

Listen to the Angels
by Ann Marie

Listen to the angels,
they speak to your heart.
Listen to the angels,
you and they are never far apart.

Listen to the angels,
remember your Source and begin to play.
Listen to the angels
and wash your turmoils away.

Listen to the angels
and know that you are One.
Listen to the angels,
let the golden threads of joy be spun.

Have a Heart

Poems have been written about it, songs have been sung; there would be no Valentines Day without it. It is one of the most frequently used words in our vocabulary: "I love you with all of my heart." "My heart cries for you." "You broke my heart." The list goes on.

Everything has a heart, a heart center, a core, a nucleus which the whole must have to survive. You know you have a heart, as does the deer, the tree, the blade of grass — yes, even the Earth. If the human heart were in a state of disease, what would it take to heal it, to bring it back into its most perfected state of being? You might ask, "What disease is it?" But the label man uses for a dysfunction or disharmony matters little. It simply means that it is out of alignment with its perfection. Bypass surgery is a temporary fix at best. "Bypass" means to pass by the problem. The problem still exists. A mechanical heart valve is a poor substitute for the real thing. And how about a "broken heart"? How many people die each year for no other reason than a broken heart?

Focus on transmuting, rather than repairing, to return it once again to its perfected state of being. Perceive it as more than muscles, arteries and blood — but as a living life form. Science tells us that the human life form is made up of more than 100 trillion cells. If this is true, then the heart itself has billions of cells that make up its being, each cell an individual life form, a consciousness with a mind, body and soul.

To bring the heart to its perfected state of being is to bring the consciousness of each of these cells into divine harmony, working synchronistically with every other cell. When this is accomplished, the colony of cells that forms the heart will quickly re-form or replace dysfunctional cells — and the healing takes place. However, keep in mind that other parts of the body may also require some attention. The liver could still be at war with the spleen, and one kidney might be refusing to communicate with the other kidney. What about those who have a greater loss of hearing in one ear or poorer sight in one eye than the other? Is there a lack of cooperation and communication between the two? Even though there might be disharmonies within the body, no part could exist without the heart. Without the heart the entire life form ceases to be.

Yes, the Earth has a heart. I invite you to expand your perception to see a greater picture — to see the world within worlds. We have spent most of our lives focusing on the smaller picture, seeing ourselves residing on the planet Earth. The Earth is a complete life form of its own. A living, breathing entity upon which we, the human life form, reside, each human an individual cell. But the Earth has an even greater role to play in the larger picture. The Earth is the heart of the universe, just as your heart is the heart center of *your* universe. If the heart center of the universe dies, so does the universe. Because of this, a united effort has been made by beings at all levels of consciousness to save the Earth from destruction.

When man became separated from the Creator, the thymus was separated from the heart. As long as this separation remains, mankind will be unable to connect to its most divine perfection.

As we fill our hearts with love for self and others, reconnecting with the Creator, the thymus expands and reconnects with the heart as one unit, breathing and pulsing together in perfection. When this occurs, both the thymus and heart regenerate, reversing the aging process. It is the fountain of youth. It has always been within us.

The thymus is called the resonance chamber of the heart. It is the center of the greatest amplification chamber that creation has ever devised, as the frequency of every thought and the vibration of the soul itself resonate and amplify through every part of your universe.

What does all of this have to do with the Earth being the heart center of the universe? If your thymus is the resonance chamber of *your* heart, where is the resonance chamber or thymus of the universe? *It is every human on this planet.* It is the collective consciousness of mankind that has chosen to be here at this time. For your heart to be whole, in perfection, your heart and thymus must be reconnected, breathing and pulsing in rhythm with the universe. For the Earth to be whole, the collective consciousness of humanity must expand and be breathing and pulsing in rhythm with the universe. It is time — time for each individual life form to be filled with love, to "have a heart," a complete heart — to reconnect once again to Creator Source and experience *the celebration of life*.

Be in Joy

by Ann Marie

To be in joy
is to be in the moment.

It is easy to fill the mind
with thoughts of tomorrow,
missing the simple pleasures of today.

Did you see the sunset, the birds, the trees . . .
or hear the children at play?
Did you take time today . . .
to be in the moment?

Did you laugh . . .
did you feel the smile in your heart,
or notice the smile in the hearts of others?

No need to rush forward,
just be in the moment.
For it is impossible to go to joy,
you can only
be in joy.

A Builder of Bridges

"**A** what?" I asked.

"You are a builder of bridges," the gentle voice said.

"You've got to be kidding," I protested. "I'm not a bridge builder. I've never even built a doghouse, let alone a bridge. I've never been an engineer or even a construction worker. I have no idea how to build a bridge. You're dreaming if you think I am a bridge builder."

"Oh, but you are," reassured the gentle voice. "In fact, you are a registered, certified bridge builder."

"Where are you getting your information, my friend? You are way off base," I said determinedly. "I've worked in an auto supply store, as a dishwasher, short-order cook, insurance salesman, truck driver, assembly work in manufacturing — but the only bridges I've ever gotten close to are the ones I drive across in my car."

"Define the word *build*," said the gentle voice.

Here we go, I thought, one of these intellectual word games. I reached for my dictionary and thumbed through the pages. *Build: construct; fashion; increase; strengthen.* "All right, now what?" I said, waiting for a reply.

"Define the word *bridge*," said the gentle voice.

In a way I felt irritated by this game, but at the same time I was excited, as if I were being guided on a treasure hunt. Again I leafed through the dictionary. *Bridge: anything that spans a gap.*

Once again the gentle voice said, "You are a builder of bridges."

There was no hesitation in this gentle voice. It was firm and final. I'm unsure where this is leading, I thought, but I have a feeling I'm going to lose this discussion. "Okay," I said, "what's your point?"

"There are many ways to build a bridge. You have accepted one of the greatest challenges of all — to be a builder of bridges. You have come to Earth to build a bridge from one level of consciousness to another — to construct, fashion, increase and strengthen; to span the gap of understanding, knowledge and information from a world of fear and judgment to a world of love and nonjudgment; from a world of codependency to a world of cocreation."

"That is a worthy goal," I said, "a bridge that would benefit mankind. But it would take more than myself to build a bridge like that."

"You are one among many," replied the gentle voice. "Everyone upon your planet is a builder of bridges."

"Everyone?" I protested. "I could understand if you said some of them — but everyone? Look around. Look at what is going on in this world. War — abuse — educational and government systems are failing. It would appear there are many who are demolition experts, destroying the kind of bridges you suggest."

"What would it take to get you to build a bridge?" the gentle voice asked. "Imagine for a moment that you are a pioneer, and you came to a wide, deep river. What would it take to get you to build a bridge?"

I was beginning to like this game, I thought. "For me to build a bridge, first I would have to want to get to the other side."

"What would motivate you to do so?" the voice questioned.

"Well," I said, "I would have to be curious enough to see what was on the other side of the river — or perhaps there was no food on my side and I knew that I would have to go across to find something to eat. Yes, I'm sure there could be reasons that I might want to cross the river."

"What if you knew there was a party of unfriendly warriors just one day's travel away — looking for you — and there was no other route of escape other than to reach the other side of the river? What would be your decision?" the gentle voice asked.

The suggestion of such a thought sparked a sense of urgency and anxiety in me. "Well, I would get my ax and start cutting down trees to build a raft — maybe even a dead tree that I could straddle — and paddle myself across the river. I'm sure that I could find a way if my life depended on it."

"Yes, I'm sure that you could," replied the gentle voice. "And now the very life of the planet you stand on is in danger from the abuse that has been inflicted on her. It is for that reason you have come to be a builder of bridges."

"But what about those who are doing the abuse?" I asked, "What about them? And the abuse seems to be getting worse!"

"Define *catalyst*," said the gentle voice.

Quickly I reached for my dictionary. *Catalyst: One that precipitates a process or event, especially without being involved in or changed by the consequences.* "So what's the point?" I asked.

The gentle voice replied with a tone of understanding, "Your world has been in a state of lethargy much too long, allowing some people to exert their rule and inflict their abuse upon others. Yet most of your world lies back and does nothing. Yes, they may talk about it, for talking requires no commitment, but little is put into motion to change it. Just as alcoholics must reach bottom, losing job, home and family before they will admit to the problem or take responsibility for themselves, so does your society. What will it take to get your attention? What will it take to get you to act? What will it take to get you to build a bridge from one level of consciousness to another? From codependency to cocreation, from fear and judgment to love and understanding? What will it take? If a gentle nudge is insufficient, will it take a smack against the side of the head with a big stick? Those beautiful souls who have shown you abuse have come to this planet as part of your bridge-building team. They are the catalysts that will motivate you to get out your ax and build a raft. They will continue to do so until you fulfill your contract as a builder of bridges."

"But you said everyone on the planet was a bridge builder," I said.

"And everyone is," replied the gentle voice. "There are many bridges to be built, and many catalysts to urge them on. Bridges in education, government, communications, healing, spiritual awareness; bridges in technology to clean up the environment; bridges from one level of consciousness to another. No jigsaw puzzle is complete if there is one piece missing. Your world would be incomplete if just one bridge builder were missing."

"Who are you?" I asked.

"I am an angel who works with you."

"But I already have an angel," I said.

"Each person has many angels," was the reply. "Some are with you all your life. Others may change from time to time as you do, bringing the lessons that you require in the moment. Did you have the same teacher in the fourth grade that you had in the second? Was the teacher who taught you algebra the same one who taught you history? You might call me a master teacher. My specialty is building bridges. I am with you to assist you when asked, to nudge you, to remind you that you are a builder of bridges."

"Okay, so I'm a builder of bridges," I said. "But how do I do that?"

"Open your spiritual awareness," said the master teacher.

"Here we go, getting religious," I said with a sigh.

"Spiritual," the master replied, "is a universal thought form that has existed since creation, long before the term 'religion.' There is no connection between the two words other than that which you place upon them. Spiritual is what you are. To open your spiritual awareness is to become aware, to remember you are the Divine Creation, and to live your truth. When you do, fear and judgment will cease to be a part of your reality and you will choose to live and participate in a cocreative rather than a codependent relationship. If it is your desire to be your spiritual self," asked the master, "who are you?"

I could feel the joy swelling up within me, a smile forming on my face as I proudly said, "I . . . am a Builder of Bridges!"

The Emerald Isle

"O gentle soul, why do you cry this day?"

"It is because I see my beautiful world so deep in trouble. It is because there is so much disease, so much pain, so much war, so much death. Everywhere I look I see arguments, disagreements, those who are bitter with their neighbors and families. I see no peace.

"I came to Earth because I was told this was the Emerald Isle of the Universe. It was here that I would find joy and peace. It was here that I would manifest my heart's desires. Tell me, O wise one, why have I failed to find that which I have come for?"

"O gentle soul, all you seek is here — and more. Walk with me and together we will look for that which you desire.

"In your despair you have walked with your shoulders bent and your eyes upon the ground. Look up. Have you seen the beauty of the clouds, so active and alive? They are here to serve you, to cocreate with you, to bring you beauty and the nourishing rain that will sustain your body, the grass and trees, the flowers and animals and all life upon this planet. And they do so in joy.

"Look around you at the beautiful flowers of every variety. They have created a display of beauty and fragrance to enhance your life; they are here for you. Have you sat under a magnificent tree and felt its love for you as it provided shade to cool and protect you from the hot afternoon sun? Have you thanked the trees for providing the lumber that built the dwelling in which you live? Your science has long understood that all things in the universe have a consciousness. Become aware as you look around — be aware that everything your eyes can see has a place in your world. Everything is here to serve and cocreate with you and yes, to provide your lessons.

"Those on your planet have offered some interesting and provocative thoughts:

- Do you see the water glass half empty, or half full?
- Do you see yourself as the victim or as the master?
- Do you view the world in a state of decay or in the process of rebuilding your planet into the Emerald Isle of the Universe?

"As you look around, how do you choose to see yourself and your world? Remember, your perception becomes your reality."

I answered, "I truly choose to find peace and joy, but I am only one person. How can I make others change? How can I possibly change the world?"

"To make others change — is impossible. To change the world — you can. No one person can force change upon another, though many have tried. One can only change oneself, if and when one desires.

"To change the world is to change yourself. Others are unable to give you the peace that you long for. It must come from within you. First you must find the love within you — it is there. You might have to uncover it by removing the fears, doubts and guilt of old thought patterns to see the beauty that lies beyond. When you stand in the radiance of that love, with shoulders no longer bent, raise your head to see the beauty around you; see the divine creation in all that your eyes behold; the water glass half full and filling to overflowing in an abundance of love; see the master that you are. See the world in the process of change, with the opportunity to manifest your new world according to your heart's desires. Avoid looking upon your world as divine love collapsing, but rather as divine love unfolding.

"You have viewed the world as you do because that is what you see within your world, your mind and your body. Look beyond and reclaim all that you are.

- Let go of your judgments
- Let go of your fears
- Reclaim your power
- Acknowledge your divinity.

"As you do, the energies of love from within you will radiate outward and touch every part of the world you live in. In doing so, you become the example that others will want to emulate.

"If every person in the world were in peace and joy and in harmony with every other person, what kind of world would you have?"

"O wise one, what is your name?" I asked in awe.

"I am called the Elemental. I am the consciousness of all things upon your Emerald Isle and beyond. I have been waiting for you to come and cocreate with me, to share with me your dreams. Together we will manifest your desires into your reality. It is what you have come for. I have been waiting for you. Shall we begin?"

Dismantling the Victorian House

I had a vision. I was watching someone with a large towing rig pulling a Victorian home mounted on a frame with wheels. I found it interesting that the truck was pulling the house over rolling meadows with scattered trees rather than over a road. There appeared to be no difficulty navigating the terrain if the driver kept on his original course. However, several people began to appear, and finally a throng of people had gathered directly in the path of the truck. After a reasonable wait, the driver became impatient and decided to take an unfamiliar course.

I watched as the truck negotiated around trees, telephone poles and guy wires, narrowly squeezing between them. It became obvious that the driver was able to go only forward with the house and was unable to go in reverse. Therefore, it was important that he pick his way carefully. The terrain became more difficult, with houses and more trees ahead. Spotting a shortcut, the truck started to head between two of the homes. I thought there was too little room to fit the rig between them. However, the driver continued, inching forward cautiously as the Victorian house eased between the two houses, with only inches to spare on either side. Suddenly the rig came to a halt. A large tree located behind the two homes and directly in the path of the rig had gone unnoticed. The rig could go no further nor could it go in reverse. The driver thought long and hard. He was confident that it was still possible to move this old Victorian home through this maze. After considerable thought, he realized how it could be done. At this point he got out his crowbar, screwdriver and claw hammer and began dismantling the old Victorian home. All the door locks were put into one box, the window frames in another, and the 2x4 studs neatly stacked in yet another location. Finally, the home was carefully and completely dismantled.

As I watched this scene unfold, I thought how magnificent the old Victorian home had looked in all its grandeur, and how inconspicuous it looked in its dismantled state. I began to see what a powerful message this vision carried. I realized that I had just received a message of something I was already aware of, but from a completely different perspective.

We have been raised in a country that we have always thought of as a powerful nation because of its strong leadership and society. However, those who seek power over others have chosen to start dismantling our society. It has been done in many ways, by creating division with conflicting viewpoints between religions, political beliefs, pro- and antiabortion constituencies, racial differences, nationalities, social class and educational disparity, to name a few. People are growing disillusioned with our political leaders and the system they have created. That represents the dismantling of the old Victorian home.

We tend to look at life and judge it either right or wrong, good or bad. But I would urge you to look beyond the obvious and ask, "What is the lesson that I am witnessing?" I would like to offer you another viewpoint.

If we are truly on Earth to experience a spiritual journey and grow, then there is a purpose to all things. In the past, society has called for a strong leader. We wanted someone we could look up to and depend on, one who could guide us, who could do all those things we wanted to avoid doing ourselves, who would take care of things so that we could buy a little piece of real estate, own a car of our choice and maintain our social lives. But recent years (for those who have been watching) have seen a deterioration in our society in education, in skilled jobs, in politics and in the increasing judgment between those categories described above.

As we view this from a higher perspective, we find that our old, powerful Victorian home is being dismantled. To me the message has become quite clear. When we look for a leader to follow, we give up our power. Society has worked hard to create conditions that would take our power away. We have become codependent on society. As we dismantle the old Victorian home, we become less dependent, realizing that true power begins when we stop following another and begin following our heart. The growth that we seek comes from within. As I looked upon the dismantled Victorian house, now in stacks of 2x4s, doorknobs and windows, I realized that it still had all of its power, and in fact it had become more powerful. It was free — free to reshape itself in any manner it desired. Yes, it could now even rebuild itself as a holy temple.

You Create Your World

by Ann Marie

My mind searched for understanding.
I felt the presence of the angels
and I drifted into peace.
The answer came as I began to write.

There is a time for all things.
The time is now
to let go of old doubts and judgments,
to forget past events and beliefs
and see for yourself that things have changed.

Are you ready to be in the moment,
to let go of the belief that the past affects the future,
to understand that thought determines everything,
to manifest the desires of your heart?

Your doubts and indecision have created your limitations.
Fears and judgments
have suppressed your creative energy.
Are you ready to let them go . . . and be free?

Worry is meditating on the negative . . .
increasing every moment
that you share negative thoughts
or accept them from others.

Old patterns are erased
by acknowledging the magical moments in your life,
and taking a few moments
to focus on the joy and love within.

Like being bathed in a balm of peace,
washing away embedded fears
to birth new ideas
into conscious thoughts,
breaking out of limitation
to set creative energy free.

You have created the world you live in.
Now is the time
to manifest one you desire.

I Choose a Safe Place at All Times

I choose to be in a safe place at all times.

It is a proclamation that I repeat often. There have been many times when this has been demonstrated, but none so graphic as occurred one winter day.

Ann Marie and I were in Portland, Oregon, and had to make a business trip to Nevada. There are two ways to make this trip. One is to travel south on the interstate highway and cross over the mountains into Nevada. The other is to go west on I-85 and then turn south. Since we would be traveling in our 36-foot motor home and towing a car, considering the oncoming winter storms in the mountains, our choice of route was important.

As our departure date approached, Portland received a severe storm that left two inches of solid ice as far as the eye could see, including over our motor home. The night before our departure the ice melted. We consulted with our intuitive energies and understood that we would be unable to travel directly south over the mountains because of the storm. However, it would be safe to take I-85 east and then turn south. We hooked up the car to the motor home and began our trip.

There was still some ice on the highway, and traffic — mostly tractor-trailers — was moving slowly. Within the hour I found I was driving mostly on ice and that the 18-wheelers were stopping to put on their chains. I, of course, had no chains, and the country was now a solid sheet of ice in all directions, including the freeway exits, which eliminated any option of turning around. My only choices were to pull over and park indefinitely or keep going forward. Again both Ann Marie and I checked our intuition, and again our message was to continue. We progressed slowly and eventually reached the two-lane mountain road taking us south toward Nevada. This secondary road had gravel spread over the ice, providing some traction as we moved laboriously uphill on the winding road. An hour later we crested the mountain and began a downgrade when we saw a sign that said, "6% grade next 5 miles."

Suddenly we were aware there was no gravel on this downgrade! Apparently the gravel trucks were unable to get to this part of the road. The motor home is equipped with a diesel engine and a six-speed automatic transmission, and although I was traveling only 25 mph and had manually shifted the transmission into third gear, it would automatically shift into the next higher gear as the engine reached maximum rpms. And each time it would do so, it would shift again into the next higher gear.

The road was a sheet of solid ice and five miles of continuous curves. My brakes were of no use to me. To apply them would cause them to lock, forcing us into a slide. My total attention was on the road and every move that I made. As speed accumulated, I watched the rpms slowly increase and felt the engine shift into a higher gear.

For five miles Ann Marie and I sat in awe as we felt the angels guide us unerringly down this mountain road, around curve after curve, without even the slightest suggestion that the tires were sliding on the ice. It was like watching an ice skater gracefully negotiating the ice. As we reached the bottom of the hill, we were traveling 60 mph and had rounded at least some of those curves at that speed. We pulled over to the side of the road, took a deep breath and sighed, knowing "we are in a safe place at all times."

I choose to be in a safe place at all times.

You Are in Control of Your Life

by Ann Marie

As I lay upon my bed in deep despair,
an Angel came to me
and whispered in my ear:
You are in control of your life;
you always have been
and always will be.

Every moment you focus upon worry and distress,
judgment and fear,
lack or limitation,
it shortens your lifespan
and degenerates your being.

Every moment you focus upon
love and happiness,
peace and joy,
magical moments and the celebration of life,
it lengthens your lifespan
and rejuvenates your being.

Close your eye . . . and think of love.
See yourself in a field of flowers,
at the beach or in the woods,
dancing and singing in pure delight.

Feel the sunshine warming your soul
and forming a smile from head to toe.

Breathe in the love
and let go . . .
Let go.

As the smile within you grows,
see yourself drifting free . . .
into the peace . . .
into the peace.

Call on your Angels,
let your imagination soar,
feel the love all around and inside your being.
Drift into the joy . . .
into the joy.

Remember the moments of delight in your life . . .
the smile continues to grow.
Like being held in the arms of an Angel,
you feel safe to totally let go.
As the gentle waves of love move through your Being,
your heart opens
and you remember the essence of your soul.

You are Love.
You are Peace.
You are Joy.

The magical moments await . . .
Let the celebration of life begin.

Where Do Dogs Go?

Where do dogs go when they die? What a profound question, I thought. How many people would even consider this when their dog passed on? My mind dwelled for a moment on the question, then drifted back in time to the beginning of this beautiful journey.

The phone rang. It was my son David calling from Africa. He had spent the past seven years in southern Africa as a game ranger, conducting elephant research. "Dad, I have a Porsche," David said. His voice was clear, as though he were calling from next door.

"You have a *what?*" I questioned.

"A Porsche. I've always wanted a Porsche." His excitement resonated through the handset.

"What color is it?" I asked.

"Yellow."

"Why did you choose a yellow car?"

Dave chuckled. "I couldn't afford one with wheels, so I got a Golden Lab and named her Porsche. She is just a puppy. I always wanted a Porsche, and now I have one."

"Congratulations," I said as we laughed.

A few months later I received another call. David informed me that his work was coming to a close and he was planning to return home. "What are you going to do with your Porsche?" I asked.

"I plan to put her on an airplane and send her to you. Because of my current plans, it may be a few weeks before I arrive."

"David, that is a 24-hour plane trip. Will she be able to handle it?"

He assured me that she was well-trained and would be fine. A few days later I traveled to the airport to pick up David's Porsche. I watched as the airport attendant brought out a large animal carrier. I signed the release papers and opened the door. I had no idea what to expect, but to my delight the beautiful Golden Lab came out and greeted me as if she had known me all her life.

It soon become apparent that Porsche knew no strangers. She was the epitome of unconditional love. The years went by quickly, and there was never any question — Porsche was family. On occasion when David's work took him in other directions, Porsche was as much at home with any family. She returned their love tenfold and was as gentle as a kitten with children.

Later David's career would take him to Catalina Island to work with children who come to camp to experience the island's abundant animal and marine life. Porsche lived in a world that had no fences. When David was called off the island, Porsche would travel a few miles to a loving home with young children, and for that period she was their family. Porsche quickly learned the country, and the island was her home. She traveled at will, perhaps a few days with friends at the port, where David frequently caught the ferry to the mainland. Everyone knew Porsche, and she knew everyone. There was always food waiting, and everyone knew what foods she ate. Wherever she appeared, a phone call always let David know where she was and that she was safe. Porsche loved the water and frequently raced into the ocean to play. Then, without notice, she would travel to spend a few days with her other family and their children before showing up unexpectedly in camp to be with her favorite person — her mother, father, confidant and companion, David. Anyone who saw them together knew it was a love affair.

Porsche enjoyed a long and healthy life, full of love, peace and harmony. With each life she touched, she left a gift — the living example of unconditional love. If only every person could for one day be a dog, to know for one day the feeling of unconditional love, the world would heal in that moment.

Where do dogs go when they die? The same place people do. It is only another expression of the soul. The soul wants to experience all that it can be. The soul is eternal. The soul simply takes a holiday, a rest before it returns for another experience. Is the life of a dog any less than that of a human? Was Porsche's life less loving than yours or without friendship or experiences? She had perhaps more than most. She didn't have to worry about taxes, car payments, or even how to earn money to buy her next meal. I would say her life was most rewarding. She has merely turned in the old vehicle, as the soul does, taking a rest to plan its next adventure. Porsche has not gone anywhere. She is with you now. You have been her gift to her — and she has been your gift to you.

An Angelic Experience

by Ann Marie

Many people watch shows like "Highway to Heaven" and "Touched by an Angel." But how many actually realize there are angels all around them, some in physical form. At times, you too may have a chance to be an angel to someone around you. These are magical moments when you listen to your heart instead of your head and allow yourself to be free to let the magic happen. I have had these occasions to be an angel in answer to another's prayer. Allow me to share one of them with you.

I awoke to the morning sunlight streaming through the window. My heart was full of joy, for today I was heading to one of my favorite places, Sedona. I took a long, leisurely bath and relaxed in the comfort of my friend's exquisite home. As I sat in the living room meditating, I asked my angels if I could be of service today. There was a tug at my heart as I was shown a vision and asked to head toward Las Vegas.

I looked at the map and calculated the distance. I knew I needed to get on the road. Even before I got out of town circumstances began to slow me down. Stopping for gas, I "accidentally" locked the key in the van. Frustrated, I looked around and discovered a locksmith right next door to the gas station.

Once in my van, I checked my map and was on my way. About ten miles down the road I realized I was going in the wrong direction. Correcting my error, I became determined to make up for lost time. Setting the cruise control, I sat back and relaxed for a long drive through the desert. Thirty miles down the road I was stopped for road construction. I waited for five, then ten minutes. Looking in the rear-view mirror, I could see cars backing up, with occupants getting out of their vehicles and milling about. I did the same and chatted with others parked close by. Thirty minutes passed before we finally got under way.

It was then I realized that I was purposely being delayed. The angels had a mission for me and a plan was being formed for me to follow. I got out of my head and began listening with my heart. Stopping at a store, I bought extra water and snacks, even though I felt no desire for food. I drove for hours, and my heart was light and joyous as I focused on many of the magical moments that had occurred in my life. I was grateful for the freedom from fear that allowed me to be easily guided by the angels, and I anticipated the magical moment that would manifest.

Shortly after 3:00 p.m., I rounded a curve in the road, crested the top of a large hill and spotted two people walking alongside the road. They were not hitchhiking, just walking. I heard my angels say, "Stop." But this stretch of the road had no shoulders, just guardrails on both sides. The traffic was heavy and there was no place to stop or even turn around, so I continued to the bottom of the hill, turned around and went back in the other direction. I noticed an abandoned van on the side of the road. Finding a place to turn around, I once again headed back up over the hill, saying to my angels, "You had better find me a place to stop when I reach those people." Sure enough, as I approached them, there was one small turnout, the only one on the hill, just large enough to pull off the road.

They looked surprised when I stopped. I asked if that was

their van on the other side of the hill. There was a look of distress on their faces as they said no. They must have expected I would drive away when I discovered the van belonged to someone else. I replied, "That's okay, please get in anyway." They were exhausted, so I offered them water and food. After they satisfied themselves, I asked why they were walking and where they were headed. As they began to relax in my air-conditioned van, Mary related her story.

"This morning my car was wrecked in an accident many miles from home. We have been walking all day, and since no one would stop to pick us up, we decided to take a shortcut across the mountains. We had just returned to the main road five minutes before you stopped. When you did stop, I could hardly believe it."

I told her that the angels had asked me to stop. She began to relax as she continued her story. "Two months ago I went to the hospital after experiencing a nervous collapse. When I returned home, our apartment was completely bare. My husband had removed all of our belongings, including my clothes and shoes, and kidnapped our two preschool children. Yesterday my purse was stolen. I have been distraught, searching for answers. Today as I walked across the desert, I had time to review my life and make new decisions about where I was headed and what I would do with my life. I asked God if He was real. If so, would He be willing to help me put my life together? I remembered my mother talking about the angels, so I asked the angels to come into my life to show me the way. It was at that time that you stopped to pick us up."

When they had first entered the van, Mary had asked if I was an angel, and I had replied, "In the moment, yes."

Her faith in herself, in God and the angels had been renewed and she knew that her life was changed forever.

She had bruised her face in the accident when she hit the steering wheel and blood had dripped onto her blouse. I could see the pain in her face, but I knew the pain in her heart was even greater. I asked her to hold the book *Awaken to the Healer Within.* Like a child, she held out her hands in delight and placed the book over her heart. She rocked back and forth and let the love fill her being. The pain began to diminish almost instantly.

She took a deep breath, closed her eyes, leaned back against the seat and let the stress release from her body. Later she told me she felt more relaxed than she had in years. With tears in her eyes, she thanked me and asked if I would stay with her. I replied that her angels would always be there to assist her, but I must be on my way. We continued to chat as I drove them 25 miles out of my way to their home town and treated them to dinner. As I drove away and saw the radiant smile on her face, I knew that I would cherish this moment forever.

It was midnight when I reached Las Vegas and was directed to pull into the parking lot of the Pyramid Casino/Hotel. As I wandered into the casino I was dazzled by its beauty. I heard an angel whisper in my ear. I dropped a single quarter into a slot machine and out rolled $150, more than enough to cover my day's expenses — the locksmith, the gas, food, dinner, with enough left over for my next adventure.

The Little Red Hen

As I drove through the countryside, I became increasingly aware of the litter along the side of the road. There were cans, paper, tires and trash of all kinds. Occasionally there was an entire garbage bag that someone had cast into the ditch. How can people be so careless? I thought.

As I entered the city, the litter became worse. What kind of a society are we creating, where others have no honor for the creation that humanity had made for them? So much care was taken to create beautiful buildings, streets, sidewalks and parks, only to have people litter this creation with their waste.

I pulled into a gas station. As I began to fill my gas tank, I noticed another car parked alongside the station. It was obvious the couple sitting inside the car had purchased a carryout meal, which they were eating. I looked on, disbelieving as I watched them in one swift motion throw a milk carton, soft-drink cup and paper bag containing several items that had contained their lunch out the side windows of the car and drive away. A trash barrel was located a mere ten feet away.

I continued my trip into the city and found my hotel. The room was clean and I was looking forward to a good night's rest. I went to raise the window and get some fresh air, only to find that it refused to budge. I called the desk and asked how I might open the window. The clerk said, "I'm sorry, sir, we maintain a closed building in this part of town. You will have to rely on the ventilating system."

"But I like fresh air when I sleep. Why would you want to keep the windows closed?"

"The air is quite polluted in this city and often we even have ozone alerts to warn those with breathing problems to stay indoors," the clerk replied. "You would not be happy if you left a window open."

I consoled myself with the fact that I would have to get along without fresh air for my stay at the hotel. I opened my briefcase and took out some papers that required my attention before tomorrow's appointment. Laying them on the table, I looked for a drinking glass and filled it with water from the tap. I began scanning my papers and took a sip of water. I quickly forgot my papers as my taste buds reeled from the taste. Again I called the desk. "What in the world is wrong with this water?" I asked.

"I'm sorry, sir, we are on a city water system. They put as much chlorine in it as the law allows, but it's pretty hard to cover up the impurities from recycled city water. You may want to come to our gift shop. They have bottled water for sale."

I took his advice. Later as I lay in bed, I called forth my angels and asked, "Who wants to talk to me about what I have seen today? I'm becoming very discouraged."

"What is it you would like to discuss?" my guardian angel responded.

"I know you have been with me my entire life, so you have seen the same things I have."

"That is true."

"Tell me, what is it about a society that both creates and destroys at the same time? It make no sense. People pay good money to hire architects to design magnificent structures and others to build them. They are craftsmen, and I know they must be proud of their work. Then others come along and deface it. Many are proud of the spacious county we live in. It has some of the most beautiful areas to be found in the world, yet people trash it.

"When I was a child growing up, no one knew what bottled water was. Now if you refrain from drinking bottled water or have a water purifier in your home, it is because you failed to get the message. Ninety-five percent of my country now warns us that their waters are so polluted, the fish taken from these waters are unsafe to eat. And the air is no better. Respiratory problems are epidemic, and I have yet to mention the pollution of the soil and food chain. And before you say I'm just some environmentalist who is overreacting, I would say I am just an individual who is watching my beautiful planet struggle with problems that were not present when I was a boy. I know there are interested individuals and groups working to change these things, but much of it falls on deaf ears."

"You have made quite a statement," my angel repled. "You are correct in everything that you have said, but there is more."

"More? Are you sure I'm ready for more?"

"The 'more' I refer to also has a good side. Lessons come in many ways and truths have been communicated in the most unsuspected ways. With your permission, I would like to share a story with you."

"Be my guest."

> Once upon a time there was a little red hen. The little red hen had three friends, a dog, a cat and a pig. Her friends spent most of their time playing, while the little red hen worked hard taking care of her house and her chicks.
>
> One day as the little red hen was working in her garden, she noticed some grains of wheat. "Who will help

me plant this wheat?" she asked.

"Not I," said the dog.

"Not I," said the cat.

"Not I," said the pig.

"Then I will do it myself," said the little red hen. And she did.

As the wheat grew the little red hen asked, "Who will help me take care of this wheat?"

"Not I," said the dog.

"Not I," said the cat.

"Not I," said the pig.

"Then I will do it myself," said the little red hen. And she did.

Finally the wheat was ready for harvest. Again she asked, "Who will help me harvest this wheat?"

"Not I," said the dog.

"Not I," said the cat.

"Not I," said the pig.

"Then I will do it myself," said the little red hen. And she did.

When the wheat was harvested, the little red hen asked, "Who will help me grind this wheat into flour?"

"Not I," said the dog.

"Not I," said the cat.

"Not I," said the pig.

"Then I will do it myself," said the little red hen. And she did.

Finally she had enough flour to make bread for a long time to come. "Who will help me bake the bread?"

"Not I," said the dog.

"Not I," said the cat.

"Not I," said the pig.

"Then I will do it myself," said the little red hen. And she did.

When the bread was done, the little red hen asked, "Who will help me eat this bread?"

"I will," said the dog.

"I will," said the cat.

"I will," said the pig.

But the little red hen was not pleased with the dog, the cat and the pig. "I don't think so," said the little red hen. "I have worked very hard while you have done nothing. I shall keep the rewards of my efforts and share it with my family, who worked hard to cocreate with me."

"Yes, I remember that story," I said, "but I have never heard the message so well as I hear it now. There are many people who want to enjoy what our world has to offer but are unwilling to contribute to making it a better world."

"It is time to focus on the solution rather than the problem," said the angel. "The problem has already been defined in the minds of some, but I would suggest that you look beyond what others see.

"Many now realize that disease in the human body is only the symptom rather than the cause. As long as society focuses on symptoms, disease will continue. The cause of any symptom is disharmony within the consciousness of the individual. The same is true for those things you have mentioned. Pollution in all forms in society is only a symptom of a disharmony within the collective consciousness of mankind. Yes, there are individuals and groups working to correct the problem, but may I suggest that the problem will continue until the cause has been corrected."

"How do you do that?" I asked.

"You have already begun by recognizing the symptoms. I suggest that you consider joining the legions of others who are working to change the consciousness of mankind."

"Where would I begin to find them, and what do I have to do to join?"

"It is unnecessary to find them," replied my angel, "nor do you have to join them, other than to join with the collective consciousness of like-minded souls who choose to recognize that all things are the divine creation, to live their truth and be the example that others will want to emulate. As you do so, you change the balance of the collective consciousness and then your world will heal.

"Be the little red hen. See the beauty in all things. Live your truth. As others look on and see that yours is a more perfect world, it will awaken a remembering within them that they too have come to be part of the collective consciousness that is dedicated to returning the Earth to its rightful place as the Emerald Isle of the Universe."

To Honor Another

Honor is a concept that has been foreign in this world for so long. It is a word that is barely understood and one we seem afraid to acknowledge. When one has no honor for oneself, how can one honor another?

Centuries ago connections of thought existed between the Creator, or universal consciousness, and the consciousness within the human being, a link, a communication system, that would allow one to know truth even as one experimented with untruth. It is like going to a movie. As you watch a movie you know it is fiction. You can discern truth from nontruth. Yet what would happen if you became part of that movie and could no longer remember truth and it became your reality?

Through time as the veils of forgetfulness descended, people walked into the movie and they became the movie. It is as if each lifetime is a movie and truth exists outside that movie, outside the lifetime in another place beyond the limits of the Earth.

Inside the movie set, certain beings have come in for short periods of time and said, "You people are in a movie. Wake up, remember and go home." Yet everyone looks at them in disbelief because they are unable to comprehend what they are talking about.

Is it possible after all these centuries that we can reconnect the consciousness, the mind, to remember truth? And that truth could actually be lived out in a reality upon this Earth? Is it possible to reconstruct a remembrance out of the dream back to the truth, to erase the disorientation, the illusions within the consciousness of the human mind? To dissolve all old patterns of disillusionment that continue to perpetuate themselves from one generation to another, never allowing the truth to stick for long? It is what we have called the Divine Plan.

It has been the pattern that if people remember, they are judged and must be stopped or put down. It is our desire that this pattern be broken. It is our desire that the hearts and minds again be filled with joy in the pure delight of working together in oneness with the Creator.

How could people commit an illicit act if they were honoring themselves and others? Society has come to create the movie. If there were no abuser, how could you have the victim? The script was birthed in the minds of man, and souls came forth to perform these roles. They are created out of the fear of becoming a victim. And now these souls cry to be free from that which they have perpetuated. We have watched the manifestation of the shadow side of the soul far too long. It is time to sever that manifestation — to remember who we are and live our truth upon the Earth.

Honor

I choose to restore my Honor.
All laws, judgments, contracts or conditions
that would interfere with my ability
to restore my Honor for myself
and my Honor for others
on all levels of consciousness,
past, present and future,
I now release
and transmute into Unconditional Love
to be returned to Creator Source
to become a positive, productive energy.

In the name of the Creator
and from the Divine Love within my Being,
I erase from Universal Consciousness
the disorientation,
the dishevelment within the consciousness
of the human mind
and dissolve all patterns of disillusionment
that perpetuate themselves
from one generation to another.
I choose to reconnect to Universal Consciousness,
that I may reconnect my mind
to remember Universal Truth,
and that Truth may be lived in my Being
and in reality upon this Earth.
To honor myself is to live my Truth.
To honor others is to allow them to live their Truth.
So be it.

Open Your Heart

by Ann Marie

Hearts open
in the sunshine of joy,
the essence of the soul.

They close
in the presence of
the shadow of pain.

You can move into
the light or the shadow
by the focus of your thoughts.
You choose your destiny . . .

Compassion

Compassion is a concept that is often described and used in an incorrect manner. The dictionary says: *To be in sympathy*, meaning to have an understanding. It does not mean to feel sorry for or to pity another being. To have compassion means to understand and honor another.

- To be compassionate is to have an understanding of the place within which others reside in their consciousness and in their being.
- To be compassionate is to honor yourself in relationship to others, honoring the journey both you and they have chosen.
- To be compassionate is to honor the soul essence and the individual expression of that soul essence in each person.
- To be compassionate never places anyone above another, but honors them as the divine creation they are.

It is from a place of understanding that we can assist one another, never placing one above another, but cocreating in creative love.

To feel sorry for another is to be drawn into the drama.
To be compassionate is to honor another
for the journey being chosen.

Do You See?

by Ann Marie

There are many in this world
who have discovered
that they resonate only with those
who come in Love.

What does that mean?
How do they perceive
what is Love
and what is not?

It is a feeling,
a feeling in the heart.
It matters little
what thoughts are spoken
if they fail to resonate
with the energy from within.

Do they walk their talk
more than in the moment
the words are spoken,
but in all aspects
of their life?

You talk of cocreation vs. codependence.
Bottom line — what is the difference?
The difference is in the attitude
with which each deed is carried forth.

Is one person placed above another?
If so, why?
Does everything you do serve the whole:
the whole body,
the whole group,
the whole world,
the whole universe?
If not, why not?

If anything you do
does not serve the whole,
it is in separation from the whole.

Do you see?

"So you want something that will bring you joy," whispered the Earth. Have you ever considered that joy is what you have come here to experience? That this was your goal? That you came to create that which would bring you joy? Think about this for a moment. Ask yourself, 'What is it that would bring me joy?'

"There are so many things to choose from. For some it might be to assist others — to be a nurse, a teacher, a physician. For others, to build a car, a boat, a home. Yet others, to make a fine wine, bake a cake, plant and nurture a garden. Some choose to write a poem or music, create a painting, sculpture, decorate their home, build a road, fly a plane.

"Many complain about the work they do, yet each day they repeat the same old pattern. If it does not bring them joy, then why do they continue to reinforce their misery? The human experience is a world of choices. If you have chosen something that does not bring you joy, remember, it was your choice. Also remember that there are no accidents in the universe. If this is true, then the choice you made was for a reason.

"I challenge you to ask, if the choice I have made no longer brings me joy, what was my lesson? How have I grown? How have I benefited from this experience? Am I prepared to let my lesson go, to graduate and move forward? Am I prepared to seek that which will bring me joy? Do I have the courage to step out of the life raft and into the boat? Am I prepared to follow my heart?

"After all, it is your heart that has told you that what you are doing no longer brings you joy. Have you not been told to listen with your heart, for that is where you shall hear your truth? Is it possible that you have come to this planet, the Emerald Isle of the Universe, to experience joy? Is it possible that in order to experience joy, you chose to experience something other than joy so that you might recognize the difference?

"There is so much beauty to be shared upon my surface. A leisurely drive through the country — look around at the beautiful fields, rolling mountains and streams, the cloud formations. Take a walk in the woods, a hike in the mountains. Beautiful soul, I would ask, what would bring you joy?"

What would bring me joy? Today I will choose to visit someone who is lonely. It would bring me joy to bring joy into that life, not to dominate the conversation about myself, but rather to listen, sharing and benefiting by someone's life experience, for I can only grow when I listen.

Tomorrow I shall do something for me. It has been a long time since I have taken time to honor myself, something I must do more often — make time for myself. Tomorrow I will pack a picnic basket, include a good book; take a walk; find some flowers, inhale their beautiful fragrance, thank them for bringing beauty into my life; hug a tree; spread my blanket on the soft grass; meditate; and call forth only that which will bring me joy. After all, joy is like everything that I seek: it comes from within. Joy is who I am!

✧ ✧ ✧ ✧

From the Divine Love that flows through my Being,
I command that all my thought forms
and thought patterns
be filled with Unconditional Love,
and I call forth only those thought forms
and thought patterns
that will bring me Joy.
So be it.

Creative Expression

by Ann Marie

Imagine if all of your creative expressions
had been supported and encouraged
by everyone around you
every moment of every day.
Would your life have been different?
Who would you be today?

Many lives have been formed
like steel through fire
by overcoming the challenges faced
in the adversities
of physical, sexual and emotional abuse,
finding self-worth
by breaking through the shadows
of guilt and shame,
finding strength
by breaking through the shadows
of insecurity and distrust,
finding self-esteem
by breaking through the shadows
of loneliness and uncertainty.

For most, life is a series of struggles,
fighting to maintain a foundation of stability
in a world where value and honor
appear to have been forgotten.

If we fail to value and honor ourselves,
how do we value and honor another?
Where are our role models?
Can the cycle of devaluation
and abuse of self and others,
perpetuated from one generation to another,
come to an end?
Where does it begin?

When you see the love from within
moving and expressing itself through you,
you will see it in others.
When you see the beauty of your own soul,
you will see the beauty in another.
When you honor yourself enough
to expect honor from others,
you can honor another.
When you love yourself enough
to stop the self-judgment,
you can stop judging others.
When you acknowledge and encourage
the divine expressions of your being,
you can acknowledge and encourage
the divine expressions of another.

The cycle of honor and value
birthed within your soul
resound in ever-increasing waves of love
to encompass the globe,
embracing all aspects of life.
It all begins with you.

The Miracle

"O Wise One, what is the greatest miracle of all?"

"My gentle friend, what is a miracle?"

Here I am again, I thought, using words that I have so often spoken without a full understanding of their real meaning. I reached for my dictionary. *Miracle: an act or happening attributed to a supernatural power.*

"I find your words most interesting," replied the Wise One. "Tell me, what is supernatural?"

The Wise One had a point, I thought. We are raised in a world where many are unable to read or write, yet we all use words casually without understanding what they mean or how those words might be interpreted by others. *Supernatural: beyond the normal; not to be explained rationally.*

"Beyond the normal," the Wise One continued. "And what is normal?"

"Normal is, well, normal, you know," and again I felt at a loss to define the word. It seemed to me that I had started this conversation by asking a simple question, but now I found that it was I who had to answer questions. Again I leafed through my dictionary. *Normal: conforming to a certain type of standard; regular; average; the standard; the average.*

"Thank you," said the Wise One. "If I understand you correctly, a miracle is something you attribute to a supernatural power, which is something beyond the normal, which is out of conformity with the standards. The next question I am prompted to ask is, whose standards?"

"I don't know," I replied, "I never thought of it that way. I guess that by this description, what might appear to be a miracle for me may appear to be something other than a miracle for someone else."

"That is true," the Wise One said. "In truth, there are no miracles; there are only occurrences happening in divine perfection. It is the absence of the understanding of the divine process that leads you to call it a miracle. Each miracle is created and set into motion by individual consciousness, and when it manifests there are those who stand in awe of their creation and proclaim it a miracle."

"I believe I understand," I said. "For example, a person who has a serious disease prays to be healed. In doing so they set into motion their conscious thought — the most powerful energy in the universe. And when that energy manifests their desire to be healed, they stand in awe and call it a miracle. Yet they received exactly what they asked for."

"That is correct," the Wise One confirmed. "In your society people have been taught that they are unworthy and therefore they believe they are undeserving of being healed. So when the healing occurs they see it as a miracle, that they have been singled out to receive this special blessing. Yet it is nothing more or less than that which they have asked for. Yes, by their standard it is a miracle, but even more than that, it is an opportunity to open the doorway of understanding to an expanded consciousness and begin to understand the divine process of all things.

"Gentle soul, you have asked a question that is deserving of an answer. I recognize there are many things that are yet beyond the limits of your understanding. Your question was, 'What is the greatest miracle of all?' Allow me to answer your question in this manner.

"In the beginning there was light. And light was consciousness. And consciousness was information. And information was light. These universal elements are inseparable. To have one is to have all. Consciousness was set into motion by thought, and thought became the force by which all would manifest. It is of little importance to know which came first — the chicken or the egg — but rather to understand that a process evolved in divine order and that all things are divine. Everything in your world and in creation is divine and was created through the divine process.

"Individual expressions of the Creator evolved — expressions of light which you call souls. Each expression would have the ability to create through thought. Universes were created, and worlds within worlds. A soul would create; then souls together would cocreate. There were no limits, for thought has no limits. Souls would choose to experience their creation. One soul would create the Earth, then a soul would choose to be the Earth to experience what it would feel like. Another would create a mountain — and then choose to experience being the mountain. Yet another would create the rain and experience that. Others would then create flowers and still others would create bees, so creation evolved like a flower in bloom. Time was endless, for there was no time; only love existed. Light is love and love is light. All things were manifested in cocreative love.

"In their desire to experience their creation, souls would create a denser form to embody the soul: denser forms with the ability to perceive their world, to see the beauty of all they had created. The sunrise, the sunset. To smell the fragrance of the flowers they created. To feel the soft grass and the cool water against their skin. To taste the succulent, sweet nectar of the berries and fruits they had created. To hear the wind whispering through the leaves, the singing of the birds, the crickets, the frogs and all their creations.

"The soul had created an instrument which gave it arms that would reach out to embrace another. Hands by which they could grasp a stone and throw it, and watch it skip across the water. Fingers that could caress the petal of a flower or the feathers of a bird. The soul had created an instrument which gave it legs to walk upon the very Earth that it had created — to run through the fields and jump over the stream that flowed through the valley. The soul had created an instrument with the ability to express the very soul itself. An instrument with a voice to communicate, to sing. An instrument that could create other instruments of endless varieties that would play and express the music the mind would create.

"A magical world evolved that allowed the soul to express itself through the human form in ways limited only by the imagination. To create clothes to adorn the human form. To create foods that would tease and satisfy the senses of smell and touch. The creative mind was allowed to create and experience architecture, automobiles, airplanes, highways and bridges. To create art through sculptures, paintings and dance, limited only by the creative mind. The life form had a consciousness and the ability to create through thought forms. It was capable of reproducing itself to continue the life experience, yet through different eyes. The human life form — a creation of the soul. The soul — an expression of the Creator.

"The human life form is more than just a vehicle to experience smell, touch, taste, sight and sound. It is a universe of its own, made of more than 100 trillion individual life forms known as cells, which work together in cocreation with an energy field of light, consciousness, information and universal knowledge that threads itself throughout every part of the physical and etheric bodies, energetically connecting with every part of creation. It is a creation that houses every experience the soul has had since the beginning of time. It embodies the emotional body, which permits the soul to experience love in physical form, to feel emotions that can be shared only in physical form, to laugh and to cry both tears of sadness and tears of joy. The human experience allows the soul to express itself in ways unlike any other in all of creation.

"O gentle soul, you have asked what is the greatest miracle of all. O gentle soul, the greatest miracle of all — is you."

Dreams

I had a dream in which I was flying. No, I don't mean flying in an airplane. I mean *I* was flying. It was exhilarating to be free of the confines and limitations of my old world. I was soaring like an eagle: weightless, without effort. There was no stress; my body relaxed, aware that my body no longer felt heavy and dense. Every part of my being was at peace.

What did this mean — my dream — soaring effortlessly like a bird, looking at the Earth below? I was no longer attached or limited by gravity. I could feel the gentle breeze as it caressed my skin, the leaves brushing my fingertips as I moved close to the trees, the sun warming my body. The colors were more vibrant, more alive than I had ever known. I could watch the animals at play, and as I looked upon a body of water, I realized that I was not looking over water as I once did, but I could actually see into it. My world had taken on new meaning.

It seemed so real . . . my dream.

I had a dream in which I could be anywhere I wanted to be just by thinking it. I was in my home town and I wanted to visit my friends in the city, but they were so far away. I had no money for this trip, nor the time to plan for one.

I closed my eyes, focused my thoughts and confirmed my desire to be with my friends. I saw myself standing outside their open front door and they were standing in front of me. As we embraced each other, I could feel them in my arms, the fabric of their clothing against my hands, the warmth of their bodies against mine, and the scent of the food cooking in the kitchen filled my nostrils. When dinner was finished and our visit complete, I closed my eyes and envisioned myself sitting in my favorite chair at home, affirming my desire to be there — and I was home.

It seemed so real . . . my dream.

I had a dream in which I was in a large building that had no doors or windows. There were many people in the building, all happily socializing with one another. My concern was that in a few minutes I was due to give a lecture in another part of town. I searched the structure from one end to the other, but there was no possible way that I could exit the building. I stopped to ask people how to get out, but each time they would just smile pleasantly and return to their conversations without answering.

Then a thought came into my mind. It was as though there was another mind within mine talking to me. "If you are the Divine Creation," it said, "you could send a message by telepathic thought to your contact at the meeting and let him know you might be a few minutes late." Of course, I thought, that should not be difficult. I have often thought about sending telepathic messages, but now was my chance to do it. I closed my eyes and envisioned the person for whom the message was intended standing before me. Then I simply spoke directly to him silently in thought. A knowingness within me acknowledged that he had heard my message.

I continued to walk through the building looking for a possible way to leave. Again an inner voice spoke to me. "If you are the Divine Creation, can you be in more than one place at one time?"

Of course, I thought, I know that I am the Divine Creation. I have acknowledged that many times. All my life I have been told that I am made in the image and likeness of my Creator. If this is true, I thought, and I am who I say I am, then I could be in more than one place at one time and in complete conscious awareness of it. I closed my eyes and envisioned myself walking into the auditorium in which I was giving my lecture, turning to face the room now filled with people. I was fully conscious of my presence, the weight of the microphone in my hand, the stage lights shining on my face, aware of the expressions on the faces in the audience. I began my presentation.

At the same time I was aware of my presence in the building with no doors or windows. Another thought filled my mind: "If you are the Divine Creation, would it be possible to walk through that wall?" The thought stunned me. My logical mind says it cannot be done. If I walk forward into that wall, I will only receive pain for my effort. Again the silent voice entered my thoughts. "You have spent your life being taught, programmed and encoded with thought forms of limitation. You have been told of all the things that you cannot do. All things are possible — *all* things. You are limited only by your belief systems. Again I ask you, who are you?"

"I am the Divine Creation," I answered. I was startled by my response.

"And when do you plan to begin to live your truth?"

I stood for a moment reflecting on the words "and when do you plan to begin to live your truth?" I knew with every fiber of my being that I was the Divine Creation. There was no doubt in my mind. As I looked at the wall I realized that everything I could see and perceive was also the Divine Creation. As I approached the wall I spoke to it: "I recognize that you are also the Divine Creation, and I now choose to pass through you so I might continue my journey this day." I put out my arm and watched as my hand, then my arm, entered the wall as if it were passing through fog — and then my body. I was standing on the lawn enjoying the evening breeze, cool and refreshing as it filled my lungs. The clapping of hands filled my ears, and I became aware that it was coming from the people inside. They were applauding me.

It seemed so real . . . my dream.

I had a dream in which I saw myself in a building. It was three stories high and covered with corrugated sheet metal. It had no doors or windows. I was on the third floor with another man I recognized as an old friend. We stood in a room about twenty feet square. There was no furniture, rugs or wall decorations. Three sides of the room had plain walls, but on the fourth there was no wall, and the floor was joined by another area twenty feet square. Looking closer, I could see it was a large tank filled with clear blue water. As I gazed into the tank, I realized I could not see the bottom. As my friend and I stood there, with no apparent way to get out, a silent message came to us.

"There is a way in which you may leave this building. Dive into the water and swim underwater to the other side. Several feet below the water line, located on the wall, you will find a dial. Turn the dial to the setting as I instruct you. You will have a limited time in which you may swim underwater to the side wall. There you will find a glass door. Push the door open and swim through into the other tank of water. When you surface, you will easily be able to exit the building."

Immediately my friend dove into the water, following the instructions — swimming under water, setting the dial, moving to the side wall, pushing the door open and disappearing from my sight. Now it was my turn. I had no fear of water. I remembered that even at the age of five I was diving from the high board. Taking a deep breath, I dove and quickly swam underwater to the other side and found the dial located on the wall. I set the dial as instructed and moved to the side wall and found the glass door. I pushed, but as I did so, water pressure from the other side pushed back. I pushed harder, but each time the water pressure from the other side resisted my efforts. Concerned that I would be unable to hold my breath long enough to accomplish the task, I returned to the surface. Climbing out of the tank, I caught my breath and collected my thoughts.

After regaining my strength, I dove once again into the water, set the dial, found the glass door and pushed — but again the water pressure resisted my efforts. The more force I applied, the greater was the resistance. With lungs bursting for air, I again returned to the surface and climbed out of the tank.

My friend was gone. There were no doors or windows. There was only one way out and I had not been able to accomplish it. Then suddenly it all seemed so clear. If I am who I say I am, the

Divine Creation, then I am one with the water — and if I am one
with the water, then I can breathe underwater. If I am who I say
I am, I can breathe *with* the water. With that knowingness, I
relaxed and calmly entered the water, quietly slipped below the
surface, breathing effortlessly, swam to set the dial and found
the glass door. Still relaxed and breathing without effort, I gently pushed the door. It opened easily! I swam through it and sur-
faced. There I found a water slide that quickly took me outside
to ground level. My friend was there to greet me and with a
smile he said, "I see that you listen with your heart, too!"

It seemed so real . . . my dream.

I had a dream, one in which I was having a conversation with
another voice that kept entering my mind. It would appear that
I was talking to myself, yet it was different. I truly was having
a conversation with someone or something else with a consciousness. "You have done well," it said.

"What do you mean?" I asked.

"You are beginning to explore your potential. Think of all
that you have accomplished."

"I think about it often," I said. "Flying, bi-locating, walking
through walls. But that was only in my dreams."

"What is a dream?" the voice asked.

"A dream? You know, it's . . . just a dream."

"Yes, but define that which you call a dream."

Although I used the word often, it was as though I was hearing it for the first time. How do you define a dream? I opened
my dictionary. *Dream: Images or ideas occurring in the mind
during sleep.* I repeated it aloud.

"And what is sleep?" the voice questioned.

"You know," I said, "what you do when you go to bed at night — you sleep."

Again it asked, "And what is sleep?"

I was beginning to feel a bit awkward, unclear of the words I have used so often. Sleep, I thought, is what everyone does every day. Again I opened the dictionary. *Sleep: The natural state of bodily rest, marked by suspension of consciousness.*

"And what is a body?" the voice inquired.

"What is a body? Is this some kind of a test? A body is just that: a body. I have a body, my friends have bodies. Everyone knows what a body is."

"You said 'sleep is the natural state of bodily rest.' Define body."

By now I was beginning to feel a bit foolish as I reached again for my dictionary. *Body: The physical structure of an animal.*

"You have heard that you are more than just a body, have you not?" the voice asked.

"Yes, that's true," I acknowledged. "I am mind, body and soul."

"Define mind," the voice said.

Oh no, I thought. Isn't there some way we can end this game? Can't I just awaken from this dream?

"Define awake," it said.

"Forget it," I said as I reached for the dictionary. *Mind: That which a living being feels, wills and thinks.* Is there anything else you would like to know?"

"Yes," it responded. "Define soul."

I was hoping it would not ask me to define humble, because

that is what I was feeling. All my life I had used words freely, as if I knew what they meant, and others accepted them in the same manner. Now I felt inadequate to verbalize the meaning of those words I use so often. *Soul*, the dictionary said, *the spiritual part of man*. "Where is all this leading?" I asked.

"Earlier," the voice replied, "you stated that you thought often about all that you had accomplished, flying, bi-locating, walking through walls, but that was only in your dreams. I led you through these explanations so that you might discover that your dreams are not separate from your reality and that your mind and soul never sleep. You are a soul that has taken possession of a body for a moment in cosmic time so that you may experience things you would have difficulty experiencing without a physical body — smell, touch, taste and so on. It is only the physical vehicle, the body, that requires time out to rest and regenerate in preparation for its next experience. But the soul continues to experience in other dimensions. Sometimes you remember. You call them dreams, but in fact they are also part of your reality, perhaps more so than in your waking state, because in your waking state you are limited by the belief systems that have created your physical limitations. What you have experienced in your dreams is your reality on another dimension. It was created to demonstrate and remind you of all the things that you are and all the things you are capable of."

"Are you saying that I can do all these things in my waking state in my physical body?" I asked.

"Yes," the voice answered, "but before you can do this, you must remove layers of old belief systems and thought patterns that you have accumulated over the journey of your soul. Yes, it is possible, and it will happen more quickly than you think."

"In other words, my dreams were not really dreams, but I was actually doing those things — flying and walking through walls?"

"Yes," the voice answered.

"Who are you?" I asked. "I have been talking to a voice for some time and I still don't know who you are."

"I am your highest consciousness, an aspect of your soul that sees your truth, your world and Creation itself from a higher perspective. I am your intuitive thought that speaks to you when you listen with your heart. If you hear a message in your *head,* it will not be I you hear, but the voice of limitation. Listen with your heart."

"You mean that I can talk to you at any time?" I asked.

"Yes, in any state of conscious awareness. You have only to ask — and listen."

"It would be easier if you had a name like Tom, Dick or Harry. Then I could just call out your name."

"Why don't you give me a name?" the voice asked. "I will respond to whatever name you choose."

"I think I like Harry the best. That's what I'll call you, Harry. Good night, Harry."

"Good night, my friend," Harry said. "Pleasant dreams."

It seemed so real . . . my dream.

Magical Moments

by Ann Marie

The Angels said,
Open your eyes
to the joy that surrounds you
and magic happens.

There is no such thing as magic;
it is only an illusion,
I said.

They answered,
Magic only appears supernatural.
It is difficult to explain.

It is the manifestation of your thought
in a form that brings delight.

It is a form of awareness,
a knowing, an understanding
of things unperceived.

It is the wonder and awe
of things gone unnoticed.

It is found in the moments
when you perceive
the beauty in yourself
and in everything around you.

When you look for the magic
and know it will happen,
it is then
you move out of the illusion
into the reality.

Consciousness

I rolled over in bed for the tenth time. Why am I still awake? I thought. There has been so much on my mind lately. I keep searching for answers. The more I understand about my universe, the more I want to know. Again I tried to sleep, but a word kept going through my mind. I could see it in front of me as if it were written on a billboard: **Consciousness!**

That did it. "Harry!" I called.

"You don't have to shout; I'm right here with you. What's up?"

"I am unable to sleep," I said.

"Really? I can't sleep either," Harry said, laughing. "Your highest self never sleeps, nor do I require sleep. Only your physical body requires rest. What's on your mind?"

"The more I try to sleep, the more insistent a word becomes in my mind. It's keeping me awake. What is this all about?"

"Very simply, when something comes before you repeatedly, it is asking you to pay attention to it. It may be a message for you — a lesson you need to complete, an issue you need to resolve."

"If I'm going to get some sleep tonight, I'd better resolve this one. The message is one word: "Consciousness.""

"Define consciousness," Harry replied.

I reluctantly got out of bed, trudged over to the bookcase and removed my dictionary. Ah, here it is.

Consciousness: The state or condition of being conscious; a sense of one's personal or collective identity, especially the complex of attitudes, beliefs, and sensitivities held by or considered characteristic of an individual or a group; special awareness or sensitivity.

"What is it you would like to know?"

"Why does the thought of this word keep me from sleeping?"

"Tell me what you know about this term."

"I hear many people using it. We talk about our consciousness, or being conscious of something. It's a term that is widely used, but now that I think about it, I suspect that many people lack an understanding of its full meaning."

"I would agree," Harry answered. "In its greater form, consciousness refers to universal consciousness. It is the totality of all knowledge. On a more personal basis, each person on your Earth is at a given level of consciousness. The level depends on their understanding of universal consciousness and the awareness of their spiritual nature. Your spiritual nature is your relationship to the Creator. It requires nothing special other than your understanding of that relationship. Take a piece of paper and draw a vertical line on it according to my instructions, and it will help you to understand what I am about to share with you."

I reached into the drawer of my bedside stand and took out a writing tablet and pen. "Ready when you are," I replied.

I followed Harry's instructions for a simple graph and the appropriate words.

Phases of Christ Consciousness

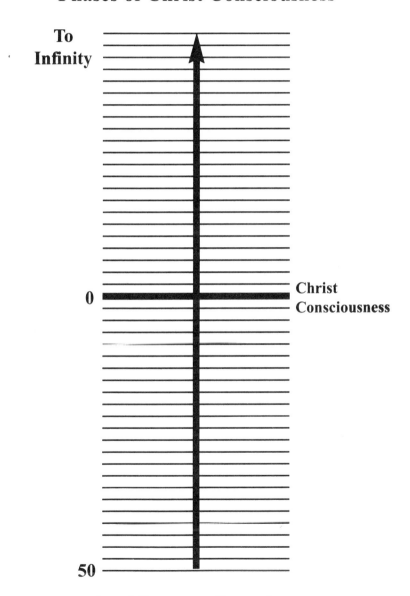

Levels of Human Consciousness

"Very good," Harry said. "This chart will serve as a simple explanation, but it should not be taken as the final word on this subject. Let us use level 50 in human consciousness to represent the point of total unawareness of the true nature of man, and continue that line upward to total awareness of man's true nature. Everyone is somewhere on that line.

• If you have no respect or honor for another — if your belief is that you can abuse others to obtain those things you desire, you would find that level of consciousness at the lower levels of human consciousness.

• If you are aware of your divine nature, but have yet to embody it into your daily life, you would be at a higher level of human consciousness, but somewhere short of the midpoint.

• If you are aware of your divine nature and have embodied it in your daily life, you have reached the midpoint — or what we refer to as Christ consciousness.

• As you expand upon that awareness, you continue to progress upward through the phases of Christ consciousness.

"Christ consciousness refers to recognizing and accepting the Christ within you. When you acknowledge the Christ within and stand without fear, judgment and limitation, you are at that moment in Christ consciousness. If you slip into fear and judgment, you slip back into human consciousness. Most people function within a range of several levels of consciousness, depending on where their focus is in the moment.

"Neither is right or wrong. Everyone is somewhere on this continuum in their journey. Consciousness differs from intelligence. Each level of consciousness spans all levels of intellect. Consciousness has to do with your awareness of who you are and to what extent you have incorporated it into your being. It is one thing to know your truth . . . it is another to live it."

"Does this mean there is a hierarchy among beings on this planet?" I questioned.

"There is no hierarchy in consciousness other than that created in the minds of man. No one soul is better or worse than another. One's wealth, clothes, profession or position in society has no relationship to being higher or lower than another soul. All souls have carefully chosen their human experience. It is through this experience that the soul grows. It is through this experience that lessons are learned.

"At this time in the journey of the soul, everyone at all levels of consciousness are moving in an upward direction. It is a reflection of the expanding consciousness upon your Earth. As individual consciousness moves upward, the doorways to the lower of levels of consciousness are closing. Mother Earth will no longer support souls who wish to live in fear, limitation and codependency."

"You would doubt it if you listened to the news," I said. "All you hear about is war, killing and more bad news."

"It would be unwise to give your energy to this kind of news. Fear has been a tool to control the masses for eons. Focus on the beauty around you and the magic that occurs every day of your life. There are many indicators of the shift in consciousness taking place. How often do you hear about angels today? How often did you hear about them ten years ago? Angel stories are ever present in your movies, books and have been the front-page feature story in your nation's leading newspapers. Be patient. You are taking a consciousness that took thousands of years in its creation and shifting it into harmony and joy in a decade or two. The shift is gradual, but it is changing more quickly than you think. You can be proud of your accomplishments.

"The day is rapidly approaching when all beings upon your planet will be above the midpoint on your chart. It will happen one soul at a time."

It is one thing to know your truth . . . it is another to live it.

As Above, So Below

"Pollution? What do you mean, pollution?" I asked.

"Gentle soul, it is my way of bringing your attention to pollution — those things that have been created on your Earth that are in disharmony with your planet," said the Wise One.

"Yes, I have noticed some litter as I travel about," I agreed, "and it seems to be increasing. Or maybe I just see the accumulation because no one takes the time to pick up the paper, cans, bottles and other items that are discarded along the roadside."

"There is a saying," the Wise One said: "As above, so below."

"What does that mean?"

"Simply put, that which you see taking place outside your world is also taking place in your world within, the universe, and is a reflection of the condition of humanity. *As above, so below.*

"The accumulation of pollution you see around you is no different than what those in your world experience inside themselves. But first let us look at what exterior pollution is. You have mentioned paper, cans and bottles. This is the obvious litter cast aside for others to deal with. In reality, it has been cast aside by mankind, and therefore mankind must deal with it. Understand that whatever has been created in your world can only be changed from within your world."

"That is a profound statement," I said thoughtfully, "but you have implied that there is more."

"Yes," the Wise One responded, "there is much more. Tell me of other pollution that comes to your mind."

I thought for a moment. "It is easy to see the obvious. Each year as the snow melts, I see the accumulation of paper and other trash that has been cast aside in the expectation that others will pick it up. Then there is water. I've noticed that some rivers seem to be dirty, and of course I hear a lot about air pollution, but that is more difficult to see."

"You are correct. Your waters upon the Earth are essential to life itself. To pollute the waters is to pollute all life forms, and that includes you. *As above, so below.* Only in the last few decades of man's existence upon the Earth have waters become so polluted with waste from industry and the carelessness of mankind that many in your society now drink bottled water or have installed water-purifying systems. Take a flight in one of your airplanes over a city where a major river empties into the ocean, and you will notice the dense, murky color of the river waters as they move out into the clear blue-green waters of the ocean. Realize that this is the water that comes into your homes and hospitals and irrigates your crops — crops that you and your animals feed upon. This also extends to marine life. *As above, so below.*"

"I'm beginning to see," I said. "I suppose the same thing can be said about the air. I know that when I fly into a city, even a small one, I can see a layer of air like a yellow cloud suspended over it, extending far beyond the city itself."

The Wise One continued, "It is the air you breathe. You know that breathing is necessary for life, yet many never consider the effects of the pollution and toxic chemicals suspended in the air that are taken into their bodies with each breath, and that many of the allergies, discomforts and diseases they experience might be triggered by the air and water they consume. But tell me, gentle soul, what other forms of pollution are you aware of?"

These are obvious, I thought; they are often talked about. Some cities have air-pollution alerts when it gets really bad, warning you to stay inside that day. "I have no idea," I said. "I believe we mentioned the main ones."

"You have mentioned the most obvious, but there are more. I will share a few that might be less obvious but are every bit as damaging, if not more so, to mankind and life in your world. Many people are beginning to write about the harmful effects of electromagnetic pollution, but only a few have noticed. It is a form of pollution that is invisible, yet it is around you every moment of your physical existence. It is silent and ever-present. Its effects reach beyond rivers or cities and touch every part of your planet.

"Remember that science understands that everything you can see and perceive in the universe is nothing more than energy. Therefore you are energy manifested in a dense form, which you call physical. You are an electrical being. Your body works electrically, and your science has long understood this.

"Many powerful electromagnetic devices, with power and capabilities far beyond those most people can comprehend, have been created upon your planet and are being used without regard to their effects on life forms or the planet itself. The inappropriate use of these devices has created much damage to life. A growing list of illnesses and diseases that mankind is experiencing has been electromagnetically induced. Your medical societies are at a loss to find a cause, yet are quick to label them and prescribe a drug to suppress the symptoms. But they do not have a clue about what caused them or how to cure them.

"I would like to take a moment for you to reflect on what I have just said," continued the Wise One. "It was my intent to make you aware of this silent force that has affected you and your world. If I have shocked you into a new awareness of a reality that you live in, all the better, for it was my intent to awaken you so that you would look at other possibilities. Allow me to elaborate further."

- Everything in the universe is electromagnetic energy.

- There are only two kinds of energy in your universe: harmonic and disharmonic.

- Harmonic energy resonates in harmony with Creator Source and with the universe in which you live. It is like a tuned piano, where every key is in tune with the other piano keys.

- Disharmonic energy is out of sync and is an interfering and irritating energy to other energies it comes in contact with. A more powerful disharmonic energy can create distortion in other energies, like a piano out of tune.

"Many are aware of the harmful effects from devices created by man. The harmful effects that have been created by these powerful electromagnetic devices will continue to exist until humans clean up and transmute this disharmonic energy in all life forms, including themselves and the Earth they live on. Cleaning up electromagnetic pollution is no different than cleaning up the pollution in the air you breathe or the water you drink. Since there are only two energies — harmonic and disharmonic — the key to cleaning up disharmonic energies is to transmute them into harmonic energy. The pollution you see around you is also in every cell of your body. *As above, so below.*

"Wow, I've never thought about those energies as pollution," I said. "We have a lot of cleanup work to do, I see."

"Yes," the Wise One confirmed. "But there is another form of pollution that affects your world and your bodies that is more devastating to life and your planet than all those we have mentioned."

"What is it?" I asked in surprise. "I can't imagine anything greater than what we have mentioned."

There was a pause, then the Wise One said calmly, "We have talked about the pollution that appears to have been created outside of you. Remember, *as above, so below.* Now we are going to reflect on the pollution that has been created within you and which in turn pollutes your world."

I sat on the edge of my chair, focusing on every word. I felt as though the great mysteries of life were about to be revealed.

"Do you remember the two energies I mentioned?" asked the Wise One.

"Yes," I replied. "You said there are only two energies in the universe — harmonic and disharmonic."

"That is correct. Mankind has been created in such a manner that it can explore all of those energies, both harmonic and disharmonic. Your minds are constantly creating thought forms to experience love in all of its aspects. You create songs, music, artwork, sculptures, games and creative inventions that bring you and others great joy. This creative energy is also experienced as emotion. Within the harmonic expressions of love no disease can exist. There is a universal law that says no two things can occupy the same space at the same time. When love is present, fear is unable to exist within this same space.

"When creative thought dwells on disharmonic energies, an energy is formed that produces toxins within your being, and as it does, those frequencies begin to resonate into the world around you."

"What are these energies?" I asked with excitement. I wondered if I was I excited because I wanted to know what they were, or because I was afraid I might find out.

"There is no mystery in what I am about to share with you," continued the Wise One. "These disharmonic thought forms are expressed as fear, anger, distrust, judgment. These take on physical manifestation in your world as separation, punishment and war. They reflect in feeling more-than or less-than, unworthy, incapable, insecure. I have touched upon a few examples; you will recognize others. Even the pollution that you see in your water, your air and the harmful electromagnetic energies around you began with a thought form. The world is simply a mirror of what you are. It is a reflection of what is going on within. Your science already knows that your body is capable of producing more than 100,000 different chemicals and that several trillion chemical reactions take place within your body every second of your life. Positive thought forms create life-sustaining chemicals in your body. Negative thought forms create life-suppressing ones."

"Are you saying that all of this has happened as a result of the actions of mankind?"

"Yes," replied the Wise One.

"I know we have to clean up the water, air, soil and harmful electromagnetic energies to make a change in our world and eliminate disease," I said earnestly, "but you're saying there is more."

"Yes. We honor those who recognize the need to make the

changes you mentioned," said the Wise One, "but we strongly suggest that before you can change the world around you, you must first change your world within. To do so is to transmute those disharmonic energies into harmonic energies. I will share a few examples."

Transmute Disharmonic . . .	into Harmonic
Judgment	Understanding
Separation	Oneness
Disrespect	Honor
Anger	Joy
Distrust	Trust
Anxiety	Peace
Chaos	Harmony

"As you transmute your inner world into the harmonic frequencies that resonate with the vibrations of the universe, the consciousness of mankind will be free to work in cocreation, bringing forth those technologies that will quickly return your world to become the Emerald Isle of the Universe it once was."

"How quickly could all this take place if everyone would put forth that effort at one time?" I asked.

"The healing would take place instantly," the Wise One answered, "and the cleansing would take more time. How long, you ask? The answer is in your hands. *As above, so below.*"

"But how do we do this?" I asked. "It seems to be an impossible task. Where docs one start?"

"Impossible, no! Commitment, yes! All that you can see and

perceive has been created by a thought form. Therefore every-thing you can see and perceive can be changed by a thought form. I challenge you to be innovative and create thought forms that will change your world. You might want to consider the fol-lowing proclamation."

My Creation

I offer this proclamation to all
to accept or reject.

I am One with the Creator.
I reach out to the Creation known as Mother Earth
as far as her energies extend
to embrace her and cradle her in my arms.
I command all energies within her Being
that have been removed, distorted
or otherwise compromised,
with or without her permission,
that would interfere with her Free-Will Choice
and her ability to experience
her most perfected state of Being,
be transmuted and embraced into Unconditional Love.
And no one shall change this proclamation
unless Mother Earth does so herself.
So be it.

Love Transcends Time

by Ann Marie

Love transcends time —
it is a symphony of sound
that echoes through the universe.
Time has no consequence,
space has no meaning.
They are only connections, one to the other.
Love joins the hearts of beings, one to another.
It is the eternal connection
to our origin.
It is God.

The Breath of Life

"I am the breath of life." The words were clear and crisp, yet soft and gentle. I looked to see where the voice came from. I could see no one.

"I am the breath of life." The words softly echoed in my ears and again I sought out their source. "I hear you," I said, "but where are you?"

"I am the breath of life. I am everywhere."

"I don't understand," I said as I looked around for the source of the voice. I could see nothing but trees, mountains and sky. "What do you mean, you are everywhere?" I asked. "I don't see you."

"You have seen me all of your life. You have known me all of your life. Since childhood you have been taught and have heard of the breath of life, but it has become such a common term, you have forgotten the meaning."

"It is true," I said. " I have heard of the breath of life, but I must admit that it is like so many other terms that have obscure meanings to me. The breath of life is even in the Bible. But this is different. I am actually hearing the words spoken to me by someone from somewhere I am unable to identify. You say you are everywhere. What do you mean?"

"I am the breath of life. I am everywhere. You have come to know me in many ways and many forms. Without me there would be nothing, for I am the very essence of life itself. I am thought. I am your expressions of thought. I am your mind, your spirit and your body. I am the trees that stand proudly before you. I am the very grass and earth beneath your feet. I am the mountains, the streams, the lakes. I am the birds, the animals and the flowers."

I stood in awe as the beautiful soft-spoken words resonated throughout my being. Every part of me knew it to be true, yet I knew there was more. "Yes," I said, "I am beginning to remember."

"Many have forgotten me," the soft voice said. "It is time to remember. Look around you and see the world you live in, a world where many have created distress, disharmony and disease. These conditions can exist only when the breath of life has been suppressed. And when the breath of life is gone, life forms will no longer exist."

"Yes," I said, "everyone knows that when you stop breathing the body dies, but you are talking about something entirely different, aren't you?"

"I am the breath of life. I am the life-force energy that flows throughout all of creation and through all forms of creation. Without the breath of life, nothing would exist. I have taken on many forms known as worlds and universes, cells and atoms, yet none would remain without the breath of life."

"You said that distress, disharmony and disease can exist only when the breath of life is suppressed. What does this mean?" I questioned.

"The breath of life is the creative energy from which all things are created — there are no exceptions. Everything you can see and perceive was created with the full expression of creative energy and contains the full expression of the breath of life. You are also an expression of that creative energy. When a creative expression is subjected to and embodies an energy that distorts or suppresses it, the breath of life, the very life force itself, is also suppressed. You have lived in a world of distorted and suppressed energies. You fill yourself with fear, worry, anger, anxiety and depression. You try to sustain your body with food that has been suppressed with chemicals and grown on depleted soil. The air you breathe and the earth you stand on have had their energies suppressed with chemicals and electromagnetic pollution. Yet none of this could have any effect on you if every cell in your body and every part of your being were filled with the breath of life."

"It all sounds so easy, " I said, "but how can this be done? I see no schools teaching people about the breath of life."

"There are many teachers among you that are offering you tools to change your world within as well as your world without."

"What do you mean by 'my world within'?" I asked.

"Your world within is as magnificent a creation as your world without. Your world within is filled with trillions of individual life forms known as cells, and they in turn have life forms known as molecules, atoms and many living forms your science has yet to name. All of these have an interconnecting relationship with each other and with the energy field that connects you to Creation itself, and it is all made possible by the breath of life.

"I said there were many teachers coming forth with tools that allow you to reconnect to the breath of life. For example, many have looked to food to sustain their life-force energy, and while food is one of those tools that can benefit the human life form, for many its full potential is never realized. If the life-force energy of your food and your life-force energy have both been depleted, it follows that you cannot use a depleted energy to raise your deplet-ed life-force energy. Eating for the sake of eating does little to attain the full potential of those who consume the food."

"How can we reach that potential?" I asked. "Many people live in a society where food is plentiful and often waste much of what is placed before them."

"First, honor the food that is placed before you."

"Are you saying we should pray over our food?" I asked.

"You may use whatever words you choose. Choose an intent that will honor whatever form you have chosen to sustain your life form. In doing so, you will raise its life-force energy to a higher potential and restore the breath of life within it. By honoring your food, you also acknowledge your own creation and allow your being to embrace and embody the breath of life that the food contains within it."

"I am beginning to understand," I said. "That would also be true with everything we would put on or into our body."

"That is true," the gentle voice replied, "but remember, the most powerful energy you put into your being are thought forms. By now you have become aware that distorted thought forms will deplete your life-force energy and suppress the breath of life. It is also true that positive thought forms can increase your life-force energy. You have put thought forms together and have named them affirmations, or what many now refer to as proclamations of the soul. These are powerful positive energies that have the potential of transmuting disharmonic energies. I have said they have potential, for the full potential of these tools will never be realized until you embody them in your inner world — completely!"

"It sounds so easy," I said. "But how do I embody a thought?"

"It is time to change your perception of creation, your world and yourself. Everything you perceive, every tool at your command, is filled with the breath of life. Your thoughts and the words you utter are the very breath of life itself. Form thoughts that will bring you joy, form them into a proclamation of the soul. Say them with intent, embrace them, take a deep breath and accept them into your world. Allow them to fill and resonate throughout your being.

"For I am the Earth, I am the Universe, I am the Creator you have so often spoke of. I am Creation itself. I am you. I am the Breath of Life."

Divine Plan

Recently a real-life drama received national attention. A 28-year-old woman in Rochester, New York, had been in the hospital in a comatose state for the past ten years. Prior to her present condition, she had been very outspoken against abortion.

The doctors described her as being in a vegetative state. She sometimes seemed able to follow others with her eyes, but it was their belief that she had no conscious memory of what she saw. She also responded to touch and breathed on her own, but was unable to eat and had to be fed intravenously.

Recently, they noticed that her stomach was swelling. Examination showed that she was pregnant. Although hospital officials were unsure who was responsible, they suspected a hospital employee who a few years before was responsible for the pregnancy of another female patient. They had asked this man to take a DNA test, but he had refused to cooperate. In addition, the girl's parents wanted the baby to come to full term so they could adopt it. They wanted this child as a living memory of their daughter. A real-life drama was unfolding that was worthy of the best soap-opera scriptwriters.

Of course, this quickly came to the attention of local radio talk-show hosts, who love to use such stories to air the opinions of their listening audiences. As I was driving one day, I listened for forty-five minutes as this story unfolded on the airwaves. The obvious questions that stirred listeners to call the radio station were: Since the girl had been so strongly outspoken against abortion, should the baby be allowed to go full term? What would you tell the child about its parents? Since this was the result of an unspeakable act upon a totally defenseless woman, was an abortion in order? After all, the parents could simply use photos of their daughter for memories or just enjoy the memories they already had of her.

I listened, a swell of emotion arose within me. Watching this drama from a higher perspective, I thought, What an incredible lesson this beautiful soul has chosen. Yes, those were my words: "this soul has chosen." Even when the body is comatose, the soul is not. After all, the soul is in charge of this earthly experience, not the body. To the logical mind, the woman is comatose. But it is important to remember that the soul is still attached to that human experience; if it were otherwise, the body would die. While the woman no longer seems to respond, the soul is conscious of all that is going on. Also, we should be aware that we create all of our life experiences and that all things are in divine order.

So what are the lessons that have been created?

> • To face the observers with *their* truth. To create a real-life situation in which the woman herself would be uninvolved in making any decisions, but in which others would have to face their truths and make *their* decisions. "But she has been comatose for ten years," some would say. But ten years is only a heartbeat in the evolution of the soul.

> • If the parents adopted the child, what would they tell it about its parents? How many children are conceived

unintentionally? How many children are conceived without any thought about their future? And how many are raised without affection from their parents? How many are conceived, then put up for adoption or abandoned? Here would be a child who would be loved. It would be cared for and nurtured by loving grandparents who would always see their daughter within this child. Here is the opportunity to tell this child that it was through divine planning that God had chosen to create its life so that the grandparents and child could share and express their love for each other.

• Was this really an unspeakable act upon a totally defenseless woman, or was it the journey of two souls participating in this many-faceted lesson by which *we* could all learn and grow? Is it not time to look for the Divine Plan in all life's experiences?

Separation

I have noticed that you spend a lot of time talking to yourself. Is there something troubling you?" John asked.

"Oh, that," I replied. "No, actually I have been talking to my highest self."

"Who?"

"My highest self — you know, my highest consciousness. I even gave him a name. I call him Harry. Anytime I want to talk to him, I just call him by name and he answers."

"I didn't know you could do that," said John. "Why would you want to talk to your highest self?"

"My highest self is who I am. It is my intuitive self, the sum total of all the experiences my soul has had since the beginning of creation. When I communicate with my highest consciousness, it is like surfing the Web sites on my computer. In fact, Harry is my Web site, and I can access all the information that is available in universal knowledge."

"You really believe that, don't you?"

"I not only believe it, I know it. I have had some interesting conversations with Harry, and he has been assisting me to understand who I am, why I have chosen this journey and to explore universal truths."

"Do you think Harry could help me with something that has been troubling me?" John asked.

"I'm sure he would. Harry," I called, "can you assist John?"

"I have been looking forward to it all day," Harry replied.

"What do you mean, all day?" I asked. "He just got here five minutes ago."

"True, but I have known all day that he would be here and that he would ask for my assistance."

"Do you mean that you can see into the future?"

"That may be the term you would use, but I would simply say that all time — past, present and future — exists in the moment. I perceive the most likely conclusion based on the thought forms and energy that have been set into motion. Unless you choose to change the direction of that energy, this will be the most proba-ble outcome. Yes, I have been expecting John. I know that he has been struggling with a thought for some time. Welcome to my world, John. How may I assist you today?"

"I'm impressed," said John, "and a bit awed by this whole conversation."

"Don't be," Harry said, "We're just plain folks like you. Tell me, what is troubling you?"

"Separation."

"Define separation," Harry requested.

"Sorry, John, I should have told you about Harry. He requires that you carry a dictionary," I said as I pushed mine across the table.

John flipped quickly through the pages. *Separation: The act or process of separating; the condition of being separated; the place at which a division or parting occurs; an interval or a space that separates; a gap.*

"And what is it about separation that you want to know?"

"Everywhere I turn, there seems to be separation. As I read the newspaper, listen to the radio, watch television or listen to people talk, there seems to be separation. I'm sure that some types of sep-aration might be desirable, but many of them disturb me."

"Name a few," said Harry.

"Well, there are the obvious ones: political parties, race and religion."

"Yes, those have been around for a long time. Can you name some others?"

"How about nationality, education and social class?"

"And what does this all mean to you?"

John paused to reflect for a moment. "All my life I have watched my friends argue over these and other issues. Sometimes the conversations become very heated, and there have been times when fights took place because of the differences in opinion. I have seen friendships break up because of this."

"This is all quite true," agreed Harry. "Can you name more topics in which separation has occurred?"

"Clubs have been a big issue. Some clubs ban women, cer-tain races or different social classes. Organizations and profes-sions often act as a catalyst to create separation. I recognize these have their positive points, that people of like minds enjoy each others' company, but when taken to extremes, it can create a social hierarchy.

"This sounds interesting," I said. "John, can I add some to your list?"

"Help yourself," he grinned.

"There are some very subtle ones in front of us every day that go almost unnoticed. At the same time it is what everyone is talking about. What about abortion or smoking versus non-smoking? Vegetarians versus meat eaters, and buying foreign versus buying locally? All of these are or have been major issues in our society."

"You have brought up a number of ways that separation is created in your world," Harry agreed, "and there are many more. Environmentalism, medical versus alternative medicine, animal activism, male versus female, music, drinking, drugs, culture, language, and even lefties versus righties. If you put your minds to it, you can add many more to the list. The number is irrelevant. What is important is, what has been the purpose of separation in your world?"

"Purpose? I didn't know it *had* a purpose," John said.

"For every action, there is an opposite and equal reaction," Harry stated. "Are you familiar with the phrase, *United we stand, divided we fall?*"

"Yes," we replied in unison.

"Have you ever heard your politicians say, 'If we can get 15% of the population to vote for this issue, we can get it passed'?"

Again we replied in the affirmative.

"The reason is quite simple. If they can get 15% of the vote, it would pass because the other 85% are undecided. *United we stand, divided we fall.*

"Often separation is viewed as something that just happens, but frequently it is planned and perpetuated. Those who choose to place their power and control over others know well the term *United we stand, divided we fall.* The greater the division, the greater the power.

"What creates separation? Anything that threatens your beliefs or comfort zone. I would ask you, John, how would you describe this subject in a few words?"

"Not honoring others — or yourself."

"What a profound observation," said Harry. "You have said

the magic word — *honor.* You could write a book on this subject and yet sum it up with the words you have so wisely chosen.

Separation — not honoring others or yourself.

"Separation creates judgment. You are either a Yankee or a Rebel; you *must* choose one side or the other. These are the rules of separation. However, when you honor another, you truly understand that these are only choices. Imagine how quickly the world would change if others honored and supported you for the choices you have made. Imagine the blessing you would give others if you honored and supported the choices *they* have made. Yours is a world of choice. Honor your creation, for it is your world. It is the world you have created — and your world can change in a heartbeat when you recognize the perfection within others and honor them for their journey.

"John, now that you have an understanding of your subject, what do you wish to do with it?" Harry asked.

"I would like to be a positive force to assist humanity to honor one another," John said humbly.

"As you explore opportunities to cocreate and restore your universe to its divine perfection, there is an area you might wish to consider.

"Humanity has lived in a world of fear and limitation, in societies that have joined in a collective effort to create and maintain control over its subjects.

"Many have come at this time to create change, each with a precious gift of love and a message to share for the transformation from codependency, fear and limitation into a world of cocreation, love, peace and joy. However, one thing is visibly missing from the greater picture of this effort. It is the unification of the *collective consciousness* of all like-minded people. It does not mean that you have to do the same work or that you change anything in how you are presenting this work. Each person has brought his or her own special gift to share. What has been missing is a link that will unite this conscious thought *as one* in the effort to move from one world into another, from one level of consciousness to another."

Mission Statement for the Planet Earth

We declare our intent to unite and assist
in the restoration of Mother Earth
to the role of the
Emerald Isle of the Universe.
We daily implement our desire
to move out of a world of fear and limitation
into a world of cocreation,
where only love, joy and peace will reside
in the hearts of mankind
and in the consciousness of all life forms upon the Earth.
We extend this energy into the universe itself
and to the consciousness of all creation.

One in Consciousness
One in Love

From the Divine Love that flows within my Being,
I honor and support those
who have committed their energies
to the restoration of the Earth
and the Universe of Earth.
I recognize that each energy
has come forth with a special gift to share,
and I choose to support those
who create and cocreate in Unconditional Love,
and that our universe be filled
with the divine expression of Creative Love.
I give myself permission to join as one in mind
and one in consciousness
in this effort.
So be it.

Imagine how quickly the world would change
if others honored and supported you
for the choices you have made.
Imagine the blessing you would give another
if you honored and supported
the choices they have made.

Morning Sunshine

by Ann Marie

The morning sunshine
brings forth the day
full of possibilities . . .

What have you asked for?

What are you prepared to receive?

The Bird-Cage Door

It was an exciting time for Rebecca and Alex. It was the beginning of a new relationship for them. Each had recently ended a long-term relationship with their respective spouses. They had endured the judgments of their families, friends and society, a society that expects you to live your life the way it wants you to, with little consideration of your own needs. But that was past, and it was time for each of them to work at making a new life for themselves. After all, life does go on.

Alex had no regrets about his marriage. It had been a lifetime in itself, full of exciting times, raising a family and enjoying the fruits of his labors. But something was missing. It was difficult to describe, and others would have a hard time understanding if he tried to explain. Something inside was unfulfilled. He knew he must create a new life if he were to find and explore all that life had to offer him. His deep inner knowing said he had yet to begin the journey upon this Earth he had come to experience.

Rebecca's marriage was one in which there had been little social life. There had been no honeymoon and they rarely went to a party or enjoyed a vacation together. The few social engagements they did have were limited to an occasional dinner with friends. If she was having a good time, her mate quickly let her know there must be something wrong. She soon found that "it hurt to have a good time." She also found that if she agreed with her husband, she was always right, but if she disagreed, she was wrong. She found that "it hurt to speak her truth."

When she entered a relationship with Alex, he told her that their relationship would be based on unconditional love. "The door swings both ways," he said, "and it swings in love." If you feel at any time you need to leave to further your growth, you may do so in love, and with my blessings."

As the relationship progressed, Rebecca became aware that every time she said something, she said it with caution, looking over her shoulder to see if she was going to be chastised. Each time she was allowed to express herself without judgment or criticism. This was scary for her. It was new territory, and she didn't know what the rules were. Surely, she thought, the time will come when he will criticize me.

Several times she thought of going back into her old relationship because there at least she knew what the rules were. Being able to express herself without being judged was a new experience. Each time she and Alex would go out to have a good time, she would end up crying, because her old programming told her "it hurts to have a good time." As time progressed, she became more open and soon she was able to express herself freely without fear.

When the relationship began, neither were certain that this was to be a long-term relationship. They knew they were being drawn together to complete their work, and once that was finished their lives might move in other directions. Their work brought them joy, and it was fun to be with one another. They quickly found they enjoyed doing everything together.

Then, as a major part of their work was coming to a conclusion, they knew almost to the day when they would be going their separate ways. Rebecca had met another man and was emotionally drawn to him. She knew that she had known him for lifetimes and she was being drawn to him to complete a journey of their souls. She and Alex would freely talk about the possibility of her new relationship. Alex was excited for her. After all, he loved Rebecca unconditionally. As the day drew near, plans were completed so that Rebecca would be mobile and comfortable. With great love and tenderness and without tears, they said good-bye, knowing that their lives would always be connected through their work.

Rebecca's new life was nothing short of magical. She traveled across the continent at will, following her angels. She knew that she was on angel duty, and would begin her trip each morning, often unaware which direction she would be traveling as the day progressed. She truly knew what it was to be an angel in human form. She would enter another's life for a brief moment to bring love, leaving them with a gift of hope. Days turned into weeks and finally into months. Each experience was also a lesson in her life. After all, she had never traveled on her own, been responsible for every moment of every day for her own well-being. She knew that she could now take care of herself regardless of the situation. It was exciting.

She anxiously awaited the day she would be with the man who had occupied so much of her attention. Every part of her was being drawn to him. She was aware that he was her twin flame. If she was being drawn to him, then he must have similar feelings. Yet nothing seemed to attract his attention. Nothing. It was as if she did not exist. What could be taking place? she thought. Everyone is looking for their twin flame. Many preoccupy themselves with thoughts of finding their twin flames, and she had found hers. What could be more right? "What is the message?" she cried out to her angels.

"You have been drawn to your twin flame so that you may truly understand the concept of the term *twin flame*," her angel replied.

"What is there to understand?" Rebecca said. "Your twin flame is that special individual who is the answer to your dreams. He is the one who makes your heart pound and everything around you seem irrelevant."

"Yes, this is true — and more."

"More what?" Rebecca asked.

"Your twin flame is truly your twin. It is the twin of your soul. It is the light of your shadow and the shadow of your light. Your twin flame is the aspect of your soul that you are drawn to because their energies are yours, therefore they are familiar to you and you are attracted to them. Your twin flame is the one who comes forth to be your teacher. While passions may run high, they are also expressed in negative ways, too. The relationship can be excitingly good and excitingly bad at the same time. Many call forth their twin flame only to find themselves in an abusive relationship. It is time to recognize and understand the twin flame, to ask that they forgive and honor you as you forgive and honor them, and embrace all bonds between you into unconditional love. For they are you and you are they. You are one and the same soul."

Just as quickly as her angel had appeared, it was gone, leaving Rebecca to reflect on the message it had delivered. Then she knew what she had to do. She closed her eyes, and in her mind's eye she could see her twin flame as she said:

I call forth my twin flame
to stand before me as I stand before you,
in Love.
I ask that you forgive and honor me
as I forgive and honor you.
I embrace you in Love
and I thank you for the lessons that we have shared,
but I now choose to embrace all bonds between us
into Unconditional Love
and embrace you into my oneness.
So be it.

As she opened her eyes, she knew that it was over. The attraction was gone. She knew that a healing had taken place in that moment, a healing of the soul. There was a peace that she had never known before. She realized that this entire journey had been a series of lessons — and healings.

Late one night, unable to sleep, Rebecca reflected on the last few months of her life. It was magical in every way. She had been free to explore a part of her being she had never known before. She had never been free to express herself or to travel at will, never knowing what the next day might bring, where she was going to take her next meal or where she might sleep that night. I have been free, she thought, free as a bird. The lessons had been profound and her experiences of being an angel in the lives of others would have filled a book.

For weeks she had been able to travel from one experience to another. Filled with joy and a sense of fulfillment, she knew this part of her journey would soon come to an end.

Her thoughts shifted to her own personal desires. What is it that I want? I have enjoyed my experience, but I no longer choose to be alone. I want a companion in my life. She looked toward the heavens and repeated loudly, "Do you hear that? I no longer choose to be alone. I want a companion in my life." She heard a thunderous laughter. It was her angels. "I don't think it's funny," Rebecca said.

"You have never been alone," replied her guardian angel. You have had your parents, your family, Alex. Even now you are not alone."

"You know what I mean," she said. "I want a companion to share my life and adventures with. How many are there that share my dreams and visions, that can truly understand me?"

"There are only a handful."

Rebecca thought about this for a moment, then cautiously asked, "How many are men?"

Another thunderous roar of laughter followed. "Less than a handful, beautiful one."

Without hesitation, Rebecca asked, "How many in the country in which I live?"

"One."

"One!" she exclaimed. "Only one?"

"Yes," came the reply with a hint of a smile in the voice.

"Who?"

"Who loves you unconditionally?"

"Alex." She was speechless. Everything I have experienced, she thought, has been a lesson; even leaving Alex was a lesson. My angels have been with me, watching over me as I carefully chose my path to the next lesson.

The following day Rebecca phoned Alex. "Alex, you once

said that the door swung both ways. Is the door still open?"

"Yes, it is still open. Would you like to come home?"

"Yes, I have a few things to complete here. I will see you in a few days."

I want to say their reunion was as if they had never parted, but it was not. There was a trust and confidence that had been missing before. There was a new understanding and respect for the meaning of unconditional love. It was a deeper love than Rebecca had ever known.

As the days passed, they found a new vitality in their work and adventures. Rebecca felt the walls of mistrust that were built with years of criticism and feelings of abandonment fall away, replaced with a feeling of peace and joy unlike any she had ever known.

One evening during a candlelit dinner in a romantic setting, Rebecca reached out to hold Alex's hand. "Alex, you once told me that our relationship would be based on unconditional love. The door swings both ways, you said, and it swings in love. If you feel at any time you need to leave to further your growth, you may do so in love, and with my blessings.

"I had lived in a bird cage all my life with the door bolted tight. A bird in a cage is well taken care of and never has to make any choices of significance. There is a certain sense of security in that. But a bird in a cage is never allowed to discover who it is or what it wants. A bird in a cage never really gets to be a part of anyone else's life. The cage serves as a wall of separation. When I met you, you gently took the cage and placed it into a protected environment and opened the door. Many times I came to the edge of the door and perched on the ledge, looking around at the possibilities, but I was to afraid to fly out. Eventually I learned to venture out and around the cage, testing my wings and discovering a new strength inside me. The door was always open and I was free to fly in and out. One day I flew out to discover the world, and to my amazement, I discovered *me*. By your giving me my freedom, I was able to find you."

The door is still open.

Unconditional Love:
A state of being without judgment.

What Is My Mission?

Everyone seems to be looking for their purpose. We often hear, Why am I here? What is my purpose? I would ask that you look within and consider the following possibilities. Remember, the world will change as you change. It all begins with you.

- *To heal yourself . . .*
  mentally, emotionally,
  physically and financially.

- *To stand in Unconditional Love . . .*
  of yourself . . . and of others
  even if you are being judged
  in the moment.

- *To assist others by your example.*

- *To assist others . . . when they ask.*

- *To know that you are not obligated to assist others*
  just because they ask.

- *To know when to say no and expect to be heard.*

- *To honor yourself . . .*
      to find time for yourself,
      to rest and to grow.

- *To encourage others,*
      but not do it for them.

- *To empower others*
      and not create codependent relationships.

- *To discover the Divine Creation*
      that you have always been.

- *To follow your heart and live your truth.*

- *To allow others to live their truth.*

The Greatest Act of Love

"O Wise One, what is the greatest act of love?"

"O gentle soul, define love."

I could see it coming. I knew better than to ask a question like this without first doing my homework. "Love," I said cautiously, "is when two people meet and are attracted to each other in a way that is difficult to describe in words. It probably would be described differently by different people."

"That is true. Many talk of love, but most have yet to truly experience it. If you were to explain love to another, how would you begin?"

"I guess the best place to start is with the dictionary," I said as I reached for mine. *Love: A deep, tender, ineffable feeling of affection and solicitude toward a person, such as that arising from kinship, recognition of attractive qualities, or a sense of underlying oneness. A feeling of intense desire and attraction toward a person with whom one is disposed to make a pair; the emotion of sex and romance, passion. An intense emotional attachment, as for a pet or treasured object. A person who is the object of deep or intense affection or attraction; beloved. Often used as a term of endearment."*

As I read this aloud there seemed to be an emptiness in the words. It was incomplete. "There is something missing," I said.

"O gentle soul, many have tried to describe love, but your language is inadequate to encompass its full meaning. Yes, your dictionary offers a few thoughts that you can use as a reference point, but even that falls short. Love is more than words. Love is something you are, something you experience. Love is the very essence of life. Books have been written and songs have been sung, but it is the embodiment of the energy itself that best describes what you are asking about.

"You have asked, what is the greatest act of love? The answer to your question might differ from person to person depending on their experiences, but I shall share one with you that each person upon your Earth can experience.

"In the life of each individual there are parents, friends, loved ones and, for many, children. Individuals become attached, creating a strong bond between parent and child. Friends create bonds through life experiences that sometime seem inseparable. There is nothing wrong in creating the bond of love, but the bond of attachment can stifle the very bond of love that you cherish.

"As a child grows, the soul chooses to strike out on its own. The greatest act of love parents will ever give their children is to let them go. As parents pass on, the greatest act of love their children will ever give them is to let them go. As friends move onward in the journey of their souls, the greatest act of love you will ever give them is to let them go.

"This may be one of the most difficult challenges many people will ever face. Parents, friends and children have been the focus of their life. 'What will I do if I let my loved ones go?' they might ask. 'If I let them go, I will have nothing. It is for them that I have given everything.'

"By holding onto the emotional bond that ties you together, a departed soul is held on the Earth plane, unable to continue its spiritual journey and growth. The child matures, but is unable to be free to express itself and explore the totality of all it is and can be. The emotional bond becomes a prison beyond which a person is unable to move. The emotional bond is stronger than any rope that man will ever devise. Many will tell you they have no idea how to let go because of their fear of being alone or abandoned. But I assure you that by holding on, you suppress the very person you claim to love. And in letting go, you will find the divine creation in the person you love. And as you do, you will never be alone again."

The greatest act of love
you will ever give the ones you love
is to let them go.

Releasing Bonds

From the Divine Love that flows through my Being,
all Souls that I call forth this day,
it is my intent that all aspects of their Souls,
and all aspects of my Soul be present,
and that this reflect through all Time and Space
and Beyond.

I call forth [name] to stand before me,
as I stand before you, in Love.
I ask that you forgive and honor me
as I forgive and honor you.
I embrace you in Love
and I thank you for the lessons we have shared.
I now choose to release you
and embrace all bonds between us
into Unconditional Love.
I bid you go in peace.
So be it.

Listen

by Ann Marie

*This day comes forth
to bring a myriad of ideas
into manifestation.*

*Often opportunities are missed
because of expectations . . .*

*Pay attention.
Stay focused into your heart center
throughout the day.*

*Listen,
ask questions of those who come into your life.
Watch for the doorways,
and when they appear,
walk through them . . .*

*Talk less,
listen more.
You have asked . . .
be ready to receive.*

For just one day
listen and receive
more than you talk and give.
It will put things into perspective
and open the doorway
to the cocreation you desire.

Smile . . .
and let the universe provide
the desires of your heart.

One Cycle in Time

"You have written a good book," the voice said.

"Thank you," I replied as I looked around for the source of the voice. I saw no one.

"Want to hear a story?" the voice said.

"Possibly, but your voice is not one I recognize. Have we met before?"

"Oh yes, on many occasions, often in your dreams. But this is the first time that I have actually spoken to you," the voice responded with a mischievous air.

"And may I ask, what is your name?"

"I am the Universal Storyteller."

"Who?"

"I am the Universal Storyteller," he repeated.

"I never heard of such a thing," I said. "And what does a universal storyteller do?"

"They tell universal stories."

"Of course, I should have known. How do you get a nice soft job like that?" I asked with a trace of envy.

"You submit a universal resume," he replied with laughter. "Everyone in the universe has a responsibility; you call it a job. Just because you are without a physical body does not mean you can lie back and stop participating in creation. The soul is in a continuous state of growth, and therefore continues to explore its creative energies. That is what I wanted to share with you today. Do you want to hear a story?"

This is going to be good, I thought. "Okay, you have my curiosity aroused. Tell me your story."

"It is not *my* story that I wish to tell you — it is *your* story."

It is a universal truth that everything in the universe is electromagnetic energy. Therefore, since everything is energy, it also has a frequency. If everything has a frequency, it has an energy cycle.

Some energies cycle in millions, even billions of frequencies per second. There are also low frequencies in which a cycle occurs once every two thousand years. Some can take a million years to complete, but there is no one on your Earth who has measured the beginning and end of such a cycle.

Yes, everything in creation is energy, and it is with this understanding that I would like to take you back one cycle in the evolution of man when your world was a matriarchal society, when women had all the power and men had none.

Men were kept barefoot, dumb and happy. They had no idea what was causing all those little children that were running around.

Then one day a spokesman for the men found out what was causing those children and he called for a meeting of all the men.

"You know," he began, "I just found out what is causing all these little ones, and I am really upset. We have been controlled and kept ignorant, and it's time that we took our power back."

They all agreed.

The men took their power back and created a patriarchal society. "We won't allow a woman President, we won't allow them in our clubs, and we surely won't give them the right to vote," they agreed.

But the day eventually came when women recognized the imbalance in the cycle of energy. "We demand the right to vote!" they cried out.

The men trembled. Here it comes, they thought. And the more the women fought to gain recognition, the more the men resisted.

"Not only that," said the women, "we want equal pay for equal work."

"This is clearly getting out of hand," said the men. But the flow of energy was too great. Slowly but surely women were being heard and concessions were made. No longer could they be denied.

"My friend, I have often heard you tell others to see their world from a higher perspective," said the Storyteller. "Even this story has a higher purpose.

"You need only look around to find that the majority of women have been subjected to suppressed or abusive life experiences — sexual, mental and emotional. Why, at this time in the evolution of mankind, would feminine energies choose a life experience with suppression and abuse? I can best explain it in the following manner, and in doing so I shall use a true life story of a man."

The man was a gentle soul, well-liked and respected by all who met him. He was happily married and had grown children. But life had not always been so pleasant for him.

His life had been one of abuse. As a child, he was beaten often and severely by his father. When his father died, he found himself with a stepfather who beat him even worse. Finally reaching an age that enabled him to leave home, he eventually married, only to find himself in a relationship in which his wife emotionally abused him, and the pain was worse than he had known from his father and stepfather. After painful months and years, he left her and found a loving, understanding woman to be his partner, and slowly his wounds began to heal.

Then one day he received a message from his highest self. *Beautiful soul, before you came on this life's journey, you and your father made an agreement. Your father said, "Son, there are many lessons, and each lesson will have a test. We are both the teacher and the student at the same time. In this experience I am going to knock you down, and when you get up I am going to knock you down again. Each time you get up I will knock you down again and again until you finally stand on your feet, look me in the eye and say, 'I am not going to take this anymore! I am going to take my power back!' And I shall reply, 'Thank you, the lesson is complete.'"*

"The Creator is neither masculine nor feminine. The Creator is the perfect balance of both energies. For the Earth and the individual soul to heal, the masculine and feminine energies must first be balanced within.

"Think of all the women who have come from abusive relationships. You have seen the groundswell of feminine energy grow as the collective consciousness of the feminine is choosing to reclaim its power. No, not to become a matriarchal society, but to balance the masculine/feminine energies within each person and the consciousness of the planet to complete the cycle of life.

"This is a journey for both men and women, for within each soul lies the divine masculine and the divine feminine. For the healing of the universe to take place, each soul must embody its perfection.

"It is for this they have come," the voice said, fading away.

Reclaiming My Power

From the Divine Love that flows within my Being,
I love and honor those
who have placed their power over me,
but I now choose
to return their power to them,
never to return.
I declare my birthright
and I reclaim my power,
and I will never relinquish it again.
So be it.
✧ ✧ ✧ ✧

My Divine Perfection

*I choose to embrace and transmute the bonds of illusion
that interfere with my ability to see my Divine Perfection.
I command that all records and memory
created to manipulate and distort my ability
and that of mass consciousness
to recognize and experience
the totality of our Divine Creation,
be removed
and erased from Universal Consciousness,
and the illusion be replaced with Universal Knowledge
that will allow me to know, see, feel and experience
the feminine and masculine aspects of my Being.
So be it.*

Wish

I had a wish the other night.
I wished I had a friend.
He would be tall and handsome,
he would be bright and intelligent,
he would be compassionate,
he would be understanding.

I have always wanted a friend
who would listen to my problems,
to my experiences,
to my excitements.
One who would be there for me,
to lend a helping hand,
just someone I could talk to.

And then one day I sat by a pond with water smooth as glass,
the clouds reflected in its mirrorlike surface.
I could see my own reflection among the clouds.
And then he appeared, just over my shoulder.
My friend became visible to me.
I turned around, but no one was there.
Again I turned to gaze upon the water
and again he appeared.
He was tall, he was handsome.

"Who are you?" I asked.
"I am the friend that you have been looking for.
I have been with you throughout your journey,
waiting to be seen,
waiting for you to remove the veils of illusion
that you have placed around you.
I am your Divine Essence,
I am the master within you."

I looked at the reflection in the pool of water.
As the image over my shoulder slowly merged with my own
and became one,
I looked again,
for now I saw the expression of peace and joy within
that was not there before.
I could see the master,
and it was me.

Oneness

"There is much conversation about the term *oneness*," I said.

"Yes" replied my master teacher, "it is time to recognize that we are all one."

"That's what I mean," I said. "A lot of people and organizations are going around saying, "We are one." Some people say that's just a new belief. It's easy to say we are one, but I'm confused. What is this all about?"

"First of all," said my master teacher, "it is a universal concept that has been around since the beginning of time. Recognizing your oneness — that we are all one — is not done by aligning yourself with a group in society. It is simply a matter of remembering."

"Remembering what?" I asked.

"Remembering that *we are all one*," replied the master.

"But that's where I get confused. My human mind has some difficulty in understanding something so complex — or is it something so simple?"

"That is understandable," replied the master, "because you have spent a good part of your soul experience practicing separation and limitation."

"Separation from what?"

"Separation from the Creator," the master said. "As a group of souls you chose to experience separation from Creator Source, sometimes referred to as the shadow side of your soul.

In doing so you have experienced fear and judgment rather than love and understanding. You have experienced depression rather than joy, and chaos rather than harmony. You have thereby created separation at deeper and deeper levels many times over. Separations in religious beliefs, races, ethnic backgrounds, political differences, differences in social values, social classes — and judgments at all levels.

"Look at your judicial systems. Look at your social systems. Look at all the boundaries and borders that have been created. You have done well at creating separation. It is the very foundation of fear and judgment. It is not right or wrong, simply an experience you have chosen. But now, as many are tiring of playing the game and want to remember their divine connection to the Creator, consciousness is shifting. In other words, there is an awakening taking place within your universe. It is time."

"Thank you, but I still don't understand the idea *we are all one.*"

The master responded, "That is a difficult concept for some to grasp. Let me begin by using your body as an analogy. Let's look at it as your universe, for that is exactly what it is. Your science acknowledges that you have approximately 100 trillion cells in your body. Each one is a separate life form — with a mind, a body and a soul."

"But I thought it was *I* who have the soul," I protested.

"*All* life forms have a soul. It is the energy, the consciousness, that connects each life form to the Creator. Each cell is alive and well, working independently yet in cooperation with every other cell in your universe. Imagine yourself being able to speak to a cell. You could ask it what it was and it could answer you. It has a mind, a body, a soul. It has a consciousness — remembered pain, remembered joy. It could tell you what it does for a living. It might even tell you its name. You would be quite surprised what you could learn from that one cell. It might even see itself as separate from the other 100 trillion cells in its universe, just as you see yourself separate from the six billion humans in yours.

"But you recognize that one cell is only one part of a collective whole that makes up your universe. You might even be aware that no one cell is any less — or any more — important than any other cell and that it is the total cooperation of all 100 trillion cells that makes your universe function. And although you have spent your life looking in the mirror and admiring one individual, in reality you are a soul acknowledging that you are the creator of a universe comprising more than 100 trillion individual life forms. Each morning as you look into the mirror, it would be well to acknowledge that *we are one.*"

"You're right," I agreed. "I never had thought of it that way. But you are still leaving me with a lot of questions. I'm only one small piece of the puzzle?"

"Yes," replied the master, "and you have said it well: 'I am just one small piece of the puzzle.' A puzzle is made up of many individual pieces. Each piece is a part of the whole, and the whole is the sum total of all its pieces."

"If the puzzle is the sum total of its pieces, is it incomplete if one piece is missing?" I asked. "What about when a part of the body is removed, such as a gall bladder? Wouldn't that make the puzzle incomplete?"

"The puzzle is never incomplete. The physical body is only the physical manifestation of your etheric body, your energy body. If you remove a part of the body in an operation, an accident or by any other means, the etheric body is still intact. The mind and soul still remain in place. This can be documented scientifically with Kirlian photography. If you take a Kirlian photograph of a person whose leg has been amputated — a photograph that shows the energy field of the body — it will show the complete body with the leg still intact.

"Let's look at a larger puzzle such as a corporation, nation or universe. Let us look at the puzzle as consisting of the people in the unit. If one person leaves, the puzzle changes, but is never incomplete."

The master continued, "In the game of separation that you have played, you have created a world in which you see everything as outside you. That's what separation is. If you are sick, you believe you must go to a doctor to become well. If you have a problem, you believe you must go to a counselor. If you wish to commune with the Creator, you go to a church or a religious leader. If you are in need of something, you ask your government to provide it for you. I honor the efforts of your doctors, your counselors, your religions and your governments. They have provided what you have asked for. But now it is time to recognize that we are one, that everything you seek is within rather than outside of you.

"You may seek assistance and guidance from others, but true healing has always been within. It is the emotional healing, the healing of the soul that you seek. The healing of relationships will never come from counselors, although counselors might be helpful in assisting you to recognize that healing comes from within. Prosperity, joy, peace and harmony will never come from society, but will only come when you recognize that these things must first come from within. And when you do you shall see your prosperity manifest, and joy, peace and harmony in the world around you. To see through muddy water, you must remove the contamination to see the beautiful coral reef that lies beyond.

"To see yourself as one with creation, you must expand your perception to see yourself as part of the whole. To truly understand that we are one is to acknowledge all life and embrace everything that you can see and perceive into your oneness. To do so is to acknowledge that you are the Divine Creation — standing in unconditional love of yourself and of others, in a state of being without judgment.

"If a snake appears on your pathway and fear overcomes you, it is because you see that snake as outside yourself, in separation. If you but take a moment to acknowledge and mentally embrace that snake into your oneness, you will watch fear change to love, and the drama will change before your eyes. If you are driving your automobile and someone pulls sharply in front of you and you feel anger, it is because you see that person as outside you, in separation. If you but take a moment to acknowledge and mentally embrace that person into your oneness, you will watch anger change to joy. The drama will change before your eyes. You might wish to adopt the following proclamation of the soul."

I am the Earth
I am the Universe,
I am the Creator,
I am the Creation on all levels of consciousness.
I acknowledge and embrace the totality of all that I AM.

"Acknowledge that you are the totality of all that is, yet at the same time an individual expression of the Creator. You are both the sum total of the puzzle and an individual expression of it. Your physical body represents the totality of all that you are and is energetically connected to every point in creation. Do you have any comments?"

"Only one," I replied. *We are one.*

Illusions

"**H**arry," I called out, "I could use some help from my highest self."

"Yes," Harry said happily. "How may I assist you today?"

"There is a word that keeps going through my mind. It has been haunting me for weeks, even in my sleep. What is going on?"

"It keeps coming up for a reason; it wants you to recognize and address it. What is the word that plagues you?"

"Illusion. That's all, just that one word. What does it mean?"

"What does illusion mean to you?" Harry asked.

"I really hadn't thought much about it, but when I focus on illusion, I think of a magician who will create an illusion to distract you while he does something else."

"And how does that affect you?"

"It makes me believe that he has completed an act of magic, that he has done something different from what I saw."

"You said, 'something different from what I saw.' Could this principle also apply to something you hear, feel, smell or experience with any of your senses?"

"I never thought of it that way, but of course it could," I replied.

"What other words could be used in place of *illusion?"*

"What other words?" I said. "I never gave much thought to illusion, let alone other descriptions." I thought for a moment, then replied, "What about *deception?*"

"Very good. While illusion can sometimes be created through your senses, such as seeing a lake in the desert, which you call a mirage, deception is done with intent. Illusion can also be, and most often is, created with intent. Now that you have thought about the term 'illusion,' why do you feel that word keeps haunting you?"

"That is why I called you. I'm confused. What does illusion have to do with me?"

"You have asked for my assistance," the gentle voice responded. "Allow me to do so in this way.

"As you go through your spiritual awakening, remembering who you are, old belief systems begin to crumble. The wall of limitation, fear and judgment are only an illusion that mankind has created. To create a game, rules must first be created, and in some cases even uniforms for the individual or team members. Then a game board is created, or playing field and instruments by which to play the game. Next the players embody the rules until they become a living part of them, for after all, they must play by the rules, or there will be penalties. When someone breaks a rule, someone gets out the rule book and says, 'Read this — it is a fact!'

"The fact began as an illusion and remains an illusion. It is the programming of the mind that perpetuates the illusion as fact."

A thought flashed through my mind. "Of course," I said, "I hear people all the time saying, 'Don't tell me what you are feeling. I don't care what your feelings are, I just want the facts.' Is this what you are talking about?"

"Yes, it is one example. Feelings come from the very core of your intuitive-spiritual self, your soul. Facts come from the pro-gramming of the mind. When people express their feelings, they are speaking from their heart-soul connection. Is there any truth greater in the moment? Focusing only on facts is to manipulate and control. It forces you to make decisions from your brain rather than from your heart. After all, these are the illusions by which the rules were created."

My mind was spinning. "Then illusion is not an occasional thing, is it? It affects many areas of my life. What are some other examples?"

"Your news media is replete with illusion. How often do you see or hear of a person or group that is under investigation for breaking the law? The information did not say they *had* broken the law; they are only being investigated. But in the eyes of the masses, the case has already been tried and the party convicted. After all, if there was not a suspicion of guilt, the information would never have been released. Illusions of this type are creat-ed often, and with intent. There are many possible reasons: to report, to discredit or to distract your attention from something else taking place at the time. After all, isn't that what magic is all about?"

"How do you know if the information is correct?" I asked.

"Always listen with your heart. It will guide you in discern-ing your truth. The mind is an instrument that can be easily con-vinced and deceived. No, I do not imply that you should not use your mind, but be sure that you are in control of your mind and never allow your mind to control you. You may wish to embody the following proclamation."

Mind

From the Divine Love that flows within my Being,
I give my mind permission
to give me reason and logic,
but I never give it permission
to tell me what to do.
So be it.

"You live in a world of illusions," the gentle voice continued. "Often it is the unspoken words that create the illusion, giving one just enough information to create a thought, then leaving it to the individual's imagination to complete the illusion. I will not be the one to tell you of all the illusions you have created in your world. That is for you to discern. However, I will share one more with you."

"And what is that?" I asked.

"You."

"Me?" I said, surprised. "Are you saying that I am an illusion?"

"Yes." The gentle voice paused. I could feel the love and tenderness in the voice as it continued, "You are but an illusion. Who are you?"

"Who am I? I am me. I am a human being. I am flesh and blood. I am a hard-working person who enjoys nice things. What do you mean, who am I?"

"Do you own an automobile?"

"Of course I do."

"What kind is it?"

I wasn't sure where this was leading, but it might get interesting, I thought. "A Ford," I replied.

"The next time you get behind the wheel of your automobile, I want you to say loudly and with conviction, 'I am a Ford.'"

"That's silly," I said, "I'm not a Ford."

"Of course you are not. To say you are a Ford would be to create an illusion that you are the car."

"That's right, so where is all this conversation taking us?"

"You are not an automobile; you are only a being in human form having an experience in an automobile. By this same understanding, you are not a human being. You are a soul having a life experience in a human form. Your body is the uniform you have selected to play in the game of life. You are Divine Creation expressed, a beautiful soul that has created the greatest illusion of all — to encase yourself in human form, creating a unique personality that identifies you from all others in creation so that you may create more illusions by which you will play out the game of life upon your planet. You have become so enraptured by the illusion that you have forgotten your divine connection. For many, however, the game of life is coming to completion as they awaken and remove the veils of illusion they have created, once again remembering their true identity."

Your eyes want to believe what they see.
Your ears want to believe what they hear.
Your heart can neither see, nor can it hear.
It knows.
Listen with your heart.

Lightbody

"Harry, I have a question."

"That does not surprise me," Harry replied. "You seem to be full of questions these days. How may I assist you?"

"Harry, more and more people are talking about *lightbodies*. It seems to be a new term that I am becoming aware of. What is a lightbody?"

"First, remember that this new term is an old term. Although it may be new to you, it is an expression that has existed through time."

"I understand," I said, "but what is it about a lightbody that makes it different than my body?"

"As you look around, you see bodies that exist and move within a third-dimensional world. This world is a world in which fear is present. The greater the fear, the more dense and rigid this world becomes. Within this world you are functioning in a body that contains carbon molecules. The foundation of your medical science is based on these carbon molecules. All of their research and diagnostic equipment is designed for the carbon-based body.

"As the consciousness of the Earth shifts, an interesting thing takes place. To raise your consciousness is to increase the flow of *universal information* that comes into your being. Some might refer to this as receiving more *love* or more *light* into your being. These terms are interchangeable. Love *is* light. Light *is* information and so on. Information, as it is referred to here, is universal truth and wisdom. As you increase the flow of these, your vibrations raise to a higher frequency."

Put simply,
fear lowers your vibrations
and love raises them.

"As love replaces fear within each cell of your body, the higher frequency serves as a catalyst for an electron transfer, changing the carbon atom into silicon. Silicon is what crystals are made of. Crystals are used in many forms by your science to transfer and carry energy, including your computers. Crystals within the cellular tissue hold and transfer energy as well. Therefore as your body moves out of the world of fear into your new world where love prevails, each cell of your body holds more light. It becomes less dense — lighter. It moves out of its dense carbon-based body into its light crystalline body."

"I know that many people no longer desire to experience fear and are doing many things to bring more love into their life," I said, "but how will this affect our world?"

"It affects your world in many ways. I will comment on a few. You are energetically connected to the Earth. As you raise your vibrations, the vibrations of the Earth itself raise. It opens the understanding of your true nature and people begin to remember their connection to the Creator. Your reality will move out of the world of fear. You will become an observer of the old world, but you will no longer choose to participate in it.

"Imagine every cell in your body filled with light, with the presence of God. Could disease be present in that cell?

"Imagine your mind filled with creative ideas instead of fear, worry and anxiety.

"Imagine people focusing on the celebration of life instead of death and degeneration.

"Imagine every creative expression being encouraged and supported throughout the rest of your life.

"When fear and judgment are no longer present, what will you choose to talk about?

"Imagine what the world will be like.

"Since medical diagnostic procedures are based on the carbon-based unit, how will medical practitioners perceive the people who have moved into their crystalline lightbodies?" I asked.

"This is already taking place. Medical reports have documented numerous accounts of finding crystals in the fluids contained in tears and blood. Some upon your planet have tiny crystals that sparkle like diamonds within their skin and are visible to the eye. How do medical practitioners view this? Most do not understand, but in time their consciousness will change too.

"A word of caution: At this time your world is in transition and still contains a broad spectrum of negative energies. As your body becomes more crystalline, you transfer more energy, both positive and negative. You become more sensitive to powerful diagnostic equipment and electromagnetic devices employed by technology. Since you cannot live on this planet and avoid these energies, it is important that you learn tools that will transmute them."

"What are these tools?" I asked.

"They are many. You are already familiar with some.

"Pure water to cleanse your physical world, laundry detergents and devices that are safe for the environment, organically grown fruits and vegetables to nourish your physical world, homeopathics, herbs, aromatherapy, music, art, essences and therapists that are in alignment with your consciousness. Workshops, books and materials that will expand your consciousness to see your world from a higher perspective. Proclamations that can change your world within and your world without. However, going within on a daily basis to immerse yourself in the vibration of love is still one of the greatest tools you possess.

"Do not judge the transformation as you move into your lightbody. It is the journey that humanity is experiencing at this time. As you embody love, cells will make that electron transfer and become individual lightbodies. If fear and judgment are present, those cells will transfer back into their carbon bodies. It can happen in the moment. Neither is right or wrong. The time will come when everyone upon your planet will master their fears and their universe and be filled with love and light — and living in a *lightbody*."

Credentials

"**H**arry!" I called out.

"Yes," responded Harry, "how may I assist you?"

"Harry, you said you were my highest consciousness and that you agreed to answer to the name of Harry, that all I needed to do was call out, 'Harry.'"

"That is true," my highest consciousness acknowledged.

"Well, there are many people called Harry. How do I know it will be you who answers?"

"There are many who have the name of Harry in your phone book. The Harry that answers is the one you dial. When you call out the name you have given me, you hold an intent in your mind. That which you hold in your intent is that which responds to your call. It is the *law of magnetic attraction.*"

"I understand," I replied. "You have responded every time I have called and you have shared some profound thoughts. But I got to thinking the other day, and I have to ask you — what are your credentials?"

"What are my limitations?" Harry questioned.

"No, what are your credentials?"

"I understand what you *said*," Harry replied, "but what I heard was, what are my limitations? Why do you ask?"

"Well, down here where I live, everyone is always asking, 'What are your credentials?'"

"And what does that mean?" asked Harry.

"It means that when I go to an eye doctor, I might find several certificates on his office wall that say he has gone to certain schools and passed various tests. He displays them so people will know that he is qualified to be an eye doctor, and these are his credentials."

"What else does it tell you?" asked Harry.

I thought for a moment, but nothing came to mind. "I'm not sure. What else is it supposed to be telling me?"

"Do credentials tell you how long the practitioners have actually practiced these skills or how well they perform them? Does it tell you if they are limited to these modalities or if they have expanded their knowledge to encompass a broader spectrum of health care? Sometimes what credentials do *not* say is more important than what they do. Allow me to share some with you.

"It tells you, 'These are the areas I have studied and am qualified in. I have agreed to practice by certain standards. I have agreed not to perform outside of those standards set down. These are the limitations within which I shall function even when I know there are more beneficial therapies available. To operate outside of these parameters could cost me my practice.'"

"That's a pretty strong statement," I said, "but I have to agree."

"I do not criticize those in your world. Many have worked hard to expand their knowledge and should be proud of their certificates of achievement. It is not the individuals that I call your attention to, but rather the system that limits their ability to expand upon their gift. It is time to see this in another light.

"In your world, you have chosen an experience in a physical body that has a physical brain. The brain is a computer and is limited to the information programmed into it. It is also limited to the computer operator's ability to access and apply that information.

"With that information, boundaries and limitations are now

applied by what you call 'credentials.' It is a process by which your society has grown. It is also a process by which your society is limited.

"Let us go back to your original question. You asked me, 'What are your credentials?' To understand my answer, you must first understand that I have no brain!"

"You don't have a brain?" I exclaimed. "How can you function without a brain?"

"Very well," Harry said, with a bit of humor. "No, I do not have a brain," he repeated. "Let me ask you, who am I?"

"You said you were my highest consciousness."

"Correct. I am your highest consciousness. Consciousness does not have a brain. Consciousness is all-knowing. Consciousness is connected to universal knowledge. When you ask me a question, I do not scan my brain to seek information. In fact, I never store information. I simply reach out and access it from universal knowledge in the moment. There is no new or old knowledge — all knowledge already exists.

"When you ask for my credentials, I hear, what are my limitations?"

"This is all well and good for you, but what about me? I have to use a brain."

"I would correct you. You *use* a brain, but you do not *have to* use a brain. You also have intuition, a direct connection to universal consciousness, so all knowledge is always available to you. Your society has been separated from this connection and many have forgotten it is available."

"How do you know if the information is true?"

"You have been taught to be suspicious and mistrusting. It is good to question your brain, for much disinformation has been disseminated and you must sift through the illusions to find your truth.

"When you listen to your heart, you establish a direct connection to the core of your soul and universal consciousness. The core of your soul is your highest consciousness.

"Imagine how your world would change if you went to those who have credentials, asked their advice and, rather than working within their boundaries, they called upon their unlimited potential from universal knowledge.

"Let me ask you, where does one go in your world to learn universal laws and greater spiritual truths that lie beyond the limitation of your higher schools of education? What great university will teach you the process of true healing? Where did the great minds of Thomas Edison, Einstein and others obtain their wisdom? There are many today and in the past who challenge the masters who walk upon the Earth by asking, *What are your credentials?* You *are* the school, and each experience is a lesson by which you grow.

"You have asked, 'What are your credentials?' and I have toyed with your thoughts to share a message. Allow me to share with you.

"My world is one without fear or judgment, a world in which unconditional love abounds. I am all-knowing and I thrive in a universe of unlimited potential, a universe that knows no boundaries. My world is your world. I am your highest consciousness. I am the sum total of every experience your soul has had since the beginning of creation. I am you. *You* are my credentials — and I am yours. You call me Harry."

To Be a Master

"**G**ood morning," Harry said.

"Good morning to you," I replied. I enjoy calling my highest self Harry. I believe he enjoys it as much as I do.

"How can I be of service to you this day, master?"

The word "master" echoed in my head. "You called me 'master.' Why do you call me that?" I asked.

"What else would I call you? You *are* a master. Each person upon your Earth is a master."

"Everyone?"

"Everyone," he replied.

"But there are almost six billion people on the Earth at this time."

"Then there are six billion masters upon your Earth. Each one is a master," repeated Harry. "Each one was a master before coming to this Emerald Isle of the Universe. If you had not achieved your mastery, you could not have come to the Earth. I did not single you out to ask, 'How can I serve you this day, master?' My greeting would have applied to any one of the six billion masters upon this planet. As a soul you have perfected your mastery many times — and now you have come to perfect your mastery in the third dimension of fear and judgment that has existed upon this Earth."

"I don't *feel* like a master," I said. "Sometimes I feel clumsy and awkward. There are times when I feel fear, and it is easy to be judgmental of others. Sometimes I have doubts and trouble making decisions. Occasionally I feel in control of my life, but at other times I feel my life is out of control. I see injustices, hunger, pain and suffering around me. Sometimes my life and the life around me appears to be in a state of chaos. To call me a master seems a bit overwhelming. The word 'master' makes me feel that there are expectations I must live up to."

"Have no concern," Harry said. "There is nothing you have to do to earn the right to be a master. A master is what you already are."

"If I am a master, why am I not aware of it?" I asked.

"You have chosen to come into this lifetime through a process that some call the *veil of forgetfulness*, a process that veils the remembrance of your mastery or your connection to Creator Source. You did this so that you might experience the third dimension from another perspective and become so involved within it that it would became a part of you.

"Each person upon your planet has come to experience being a master in this dimension — some to become a master teacher, others to be master cooks, caretakers, healers, soldiers, house-wives, bankers. Still others have come to experience mastery in the most unsuspecting ways — to master limitation by being a paraplegic, a beggar or a homeless person.

"All masters have chosen their journey carefully. If you try to interfere with that journey, most will resist you. You may offer assistance when and if they ask for it, but do not be surprised if they reject you when you try to force change upon them. After all, they are masters, too. Honor them for their choice. Is one actor in a play less important than any other? They have come to experience what it would be to play that role." Harry waited for me to digest this.

"But what about myself?" I asked. "Why do I struggle in my confusion?"

"Before you can master the game of life, you must first recognize what you desire to become a master of," Harry said. "You have mentioned fear, judgment, doubt, indecision and said that sometimes you feel out of control. This would seem to be a good place to start. You have doubts and indecision because there is conflict between your head and your heart. Your world has worked hard to keep you listening to its messages with your head, because as long as you do, you can be controlled by those who chose that game. Remember, they are masters, too. The game is to control you with logic — the limitations of scientific data and facts that are merely illusions.

"And how about fear?" Harry continued. "Do you hide your valuables, lock your car, secure your house, buy insurance and wear seat belts? You do so usually out of fear. How many businesses and homes have steel bars on their windows and burglar alarms? The order of the day is more law enforcement in most cities. Much of your advertising and purchases are based on fear — fear that if you don't buy the right foods, you can be harmed. Buy the right clothes and car, or you won't be accepted by your friends and so on. It is time to listen with your heart."

"Harry, you have just described my life and the world I live in, but where do I begin to reclaim my mastery?"

"What do you desire to become a master of?" he asked.

"I want to be the master of my life. I no longer desire to live in fear or be judgmental," I said. "I want to be in control — positive about myself and my actions, free from doubting my decisions; trusting, confident in my discernment of the intent of others. I want to feel safe and invulnerable. I want to employ myself in that which will bring me joy. I want to prosper so that I can enjoy my life and share with others. It's easy to say these things, but how do I make them a reality?"

"By declaring them as your own."

There was a long pause as I waited for him to continue. He did not. His statement was direct and final. When I could see that he was waiting for me, I interrupted the silence. "Declare them as my own? That's all?"

"Yes," he said. "Nothing shall be yours until you declare your intent and claim it as your own. Own it with every part of your being.

"To experience fear, judgment and doubt, you have played the role of the victim. To be the victim is to see everything outside of yourself, giving you a reason to blame others and blame circumstances beyond your control for your failures and misfortunes. To be the victim is to give your power away to others — to believe that others are responsible for your health, your livelihood, your food, your security. To be the victim is to strip away every part of your conscious awareness of your divine being. To be a master is to reverse this process and realize that everything you seek is within."

I could feel the excitement racing through my being. It felt right — I could almost taste it — but somehow it still seemed elusive. "How can I manifest this as my own?"

"You have already begun," he said. "By declaring your intent you have put thought into motion — thought that resonates through universal consciousness — to begin the process that will manifest your desire. But may I also offer you another suggestion?"

"Yes, please do," I said eagerly.

"Enforce your desires by becoming more specific. In the past it has been suggested that you say affirmations to reinforce that which you want in your life. It was a gentle way of showing you how mastery works. But now I am going to suggest that you no longer look upon them as simply affirmations, but rather *Proclamations of the Soul.* There are those upon your planet who have formed proclamations to assist you in reinforcing your desires to reclaim your mastery. If they feel right, use them. Follow your heart — be the master."

Proclamations of the Soul

Words are powerful, and I recommend that no one say words without first understanding the intent of those words. Many utter words with no concept of their meaning. Every thought is a proclamation that resonates throughout your being. The following proclamation has been repeated here to assure that only those words aligned with your highest consciousness will be accepted and manifested into your reality.

Aligning My Highest Consciousness

All proclamations that I say this day and each day,
I will accept only those
that are in alignment with my Highest Consciousness.
So be it.

Intent

From the Divine Love that flows within my Being,
It is my desire to be Well, Whole and Perfect
in Mind, Body and Soul.
It is my intent that all proclamations that I say this day,
and each day,
reflect through all Time and Space and Beyond,
before, between and after Time and Space
and on all levels of my Being.
I call forth the nucleus of my Being,
the very core of my Wholeness,
to integrate with me in Unconditional Love
in Mind, Body and Spirit to accept this Healing.
So be it.

Releasing Judgments

From the Divine Love within my Being,
whatever laws I have owned,
whatever beliefs I may have,
whatever vows I have made,
whatever contracts or agreements I have made
and those I have made them with,
through all Time and Space and Beyond
and on all levels of my Being,
that have created these judgments within my being
that have separated me from Joy,
I now release
and transmute into Unconditional Love
and embrace into my Oneness.
So be it.

Releasing Fears

Whatever fears I may have,
I know I have experienced them before.
And since I have known them before,
I choose not to experience them again.
I now choose to forgive all my fears
and all my reactions to those fears.
So be it.

Doubt and Indecision

I command that all thought patterns and energy systems
created on all dimensions
and through all levels of consciousness
that would create doubt and indecision
or otherwise interfere with my ability
or that of mass consciousness
to move from one level of consciousness to another,
now be broken and erased from Universal Consciousness.
So be it.

Prosperity

From the Divine Love that flows within my Being,
Whatever vows of poverty I own,
whatever laws, thought forms or energies that I may have
that would interfere with my ability
to manifest prosperity according to my heart's desire,
I embrace into my Oneness in Unconditional Love.
I now call forth my abundance and prosperity
in all things that bring me joy

and embrace it into every aspect of my Being
in cocreation with the Universe.
And no one shall change this proclamation
until I do so of my own Free-Will Choice.
So be it.

Acknowledge My Creation

From the Divine Love that flows within my Being,
I call forth every cell in my body
and every vibration of my Being
to stand before me now as I stand before you, in Love.
I acknowledge my Love for you.
I acknowledge the hard work you have performed
to support me in my journey.
I now choose, and I ask you
to align yourself with the Nucleus of my Being
in Divine Perfection according to my desires,
to integrate with me
in Mind, Body and Spirit
as I move forward now in my journey.
So be it.

"Does being a master mean that I have to go around being a saint?" I asked.

"Being a master is to be totally in charge of every moment of your journey; to no longer be controlled by others; to realize and experience your ability to manifest that which you desire. It is one thing to be told it is possible to manifest. It is quite another to know with every part of your being — without doubt, without question — that you are a master and that by your intent you can call forth and manifest that which you desire, knowing that it shall be so.

"There is a saying upon your Earth, 'I will believe it when I see it.' Yet others have said, 'I will see it when I believe it.' Each statement has truth. One is a statement of limitation, the other the doorway to manifestation. Which one do you choose? If you choose to walk around as a saint, what would you do? How would you act? Would you pretend to be something others expect you to be rather than that which you are?

"To be a master is to walk your truth. It is easy to talk your truth, but quite another to live it. To be a master is to live your truth. To be a master is to honor all other masters for the journey they have chosen. To be a master is not to violate the free-will choice of another. To be a master is to allow no other to violate your free-will choice. To be a master is to be in nonjudgment of another, even though they might be judging you in the moment. To be a master is to see the perfection within all that you can see and perceive."

"But what you are saying is that I must live the life of Christ," I protested.

"What I have just said," the master replied, "is that to be the master is to recognize that you *are* the Christ. The term 'Christ' has no religious connection or boundaries. It is the universal term for the divine creation of all things. It is recognizing and accepting the perfect balance of the energies that flow through every part of creation."

Being the Christ is to acknowledge your divinity
and the divinity of others.
Being the master is to live your truth.

Light

by Ann Marie

Love shines its light
from every corner of the Universe.
To move out of the shadows
and into the light,
look away from all things outside
and embrace the love within.
Choose to see only the light of love
and recognize the love within others.
You will discover that the shadows
were only illusions within the light,
illusions to react and interplay
with the illusions of others.

Choosing to see only the light,
the shadows fade
and disappear.
The light shines clear,
free to act and interplay
with the light of love
in others.

Looking at a field of light
with only one tiny shadow,
why focus on the shadow
if it will disappear when you focus on the light?

I Wonder

I wonder a lot these days. I wonder about all the possibilities. It all began when I tried to describe my world to a friend. My world extends a few houses down the street to where my children live and occasionally into town, including a few familiar stores I frequent. But mostly it extends to the edge of my property that contains my well-decorated home, a yard and several large trees.

Often I would look beyond my world and be aware of others living in a world beyond mine, a world filled with joy and freedom. But it seemed so far removed from my world. There were no fences around my world, yet I seemed trapped behind walls of old thought patterns and routines that would prohibit me from moving beyond the limitations I had created. Each day was much like the day before, and I knew that tomorrow would bring more of the same. I was caught up in my personal world and was unable to see the world beyond.

This day, however, I decided to take a blanket, place it on the ground under one of the beautiful trees in the yard and lie down to enjoy the gentle, warm breeze on this summer afternoon. As I sipped a refreshing drink from my glass, my gaze came across an ant moving across the blanket next to me.

How free it seemed to be, I thought. So free to move about, free to move in any direction, not limited by society, free of judgment from others. It was as if I had seen an ant for the first time. I wondered, How would an ant explain me to another ant?

It was an awesome thought. All my life I had seen ants, occasionally stopping to watch as they busily went about their work, but I never took time to actually understand them or their world. They are living beings like myself, I thought. Are they any more or less important than I am? I realized that I had become so focused on my own dramas and limitations that I was unable to see other worlds around me.

Again I looked at the ant. How would I explain you to my friends? I am unable to understand how you think or what you think about. Do you feel love for your fellow ants? Do you have emotions? And how could you ever explain me to your world? Are you even aware I exist? Something distracted my attention and I turned to look at the blue jay that landed on a branch nearby. It seemed to ignore me as it looked around for food. It was beautiful with its blue feathers and wings by which it could fly with ease anywhere it wished to go. Their world seemed so uncomplicated compared to mine, without restrictions.

Again the thought entered my mind, Do I really understand their world? How could I possibly explain a bird, a blue jay, to my friends? Do I really know how they feel or think? The life of a blue jay would be much different from that of an eagle or a swan. Just the thought of this made my mind spin. It was as if I had just awakened for the first time and discovered a world beyond mine. Of course I had been aware of these things all my life, but I had never *known* them.

My eyes moved to a caterpillar moving up the trunk of the tree. Yes, I thought, the caterpillar makes a cocoon and turns into a beautiful butterfly. I wondered if either would be aware of my presence. As I watched the caterpillar, I became aware of the tree itself. Is it alive? Of course.

Trees are living things, no less than any other form of creation. How would I explain a tree to another person? Do trees have feelings? Emotions? How could I possibly know? I have read stories of people who talk to plants and trees and of others who play music to them. The trees would respond by being healthier and more vital than those without that experience. How could I possibly understand the thoughts and feelings of a tree? I know that when I hug a tree I am overcome by a feeling of warmth and peace. It is like sitting on my blanket underneath its beautiful leaves, feeling cool and protected from the hot afternoon sun. Does the tree feel that same sense of peace that I do? I can only wonder.

I lay back on my blanket, gazing through the leaves above me into the sky at the billowy white clouds! What beautiful clouds, I thought. Do they have feelings? I read where science acknowledges that everything in creation has a consciousness. If that were true, clouds would also be living energy. My eyes closed and I wondered about the possibilities. How many species of animals, insects, plants, trees, fish and marine life forms are there on this planet? Millions? Billions? Does any one of them know that I am here? How would they see me? How would they begin to describe me to their own kind? Wondrous thoughts raced through my mind as I lay on my blanket and drifted into a deep, peaceful sleep.

I was awakened by the cool, gentle breeze that caressed my face. I could see nothing. I blinked my eyes again, and only then did I realize it was night. My eyes quickly adjusted to the darkness and the sky became alive with brilliant stars, twinkling as if to say "I know you are there. I can feel your presence." A sense of peace filled my body as I realized my world was much larger than I had thought. These were my stars and this was my sky. So near, yet so far. How can you really explain a star? I wondered. They are much more than just a twinkle in your eye. They must be enormous. Do they contain life? Science says all things contain living energy, therefore all forms must contain life, perhaps life forms we have yet to discover.

I gazed into the vast darkness filled with limitless stars, aware that I could see only a small part of the universe I lived in. All my life I had heard about stars, planets and galaxies that make up the universe I live in, yet I have had no conception how big my universe is. I have been told that this is but one of billions of universes within creation, yet I had limited my world to a few blocks from my house. I realized that I had created my own prison with fences made from limitations of fears and judgments. I stretched, taking a deep breath, filling my lungs with the refreshing cool night air. I felt as if I had experienced the breath of life for the very first time. The air was alive and I felt exhilarated.

Picking up my blanket, I returned to the house. A few moments later I slid between the covers of my bed and pulled the blanket around me, feeling warm and secure. I reflected on my day and knew that my life would never be the same again. I would no longer allow fears and judgments to limit my world. I want to explore my world. I want to explore creation itself and let each day be the beginning of a new adventure.

Tomorrow I am going to hug a tree, talk to that blue jay and share my joy with others as I walk down a new street each day. I closed my eyes, visions racing through my mind as I wondered about all the possibilities.

I wonder a lot these days.

Tithing

I glanced at my watch. It was 4:30 in the afternoon. The paperwork had accumulated on my desk while I had been out of town on my business trip. I continued working, occasionally looking out my office window. It was a beautiful autumn day. The leaves were beginning to turn color. What a great day to be golfing . . . but that will have to wait. There is simply too much work to be done.

The bell sounded. That would mean it was five o'clock and the factory workers would be going home along with most of the office staff. I waved good-bye to Lois and Jerry as they passed my office. "What are you going to do tonight?" I shouted at Jerry as he left. "Going fishing," he replied. "Wouldn't want to miss an opportunity like this. The weather's great . . . see you tomorrow."

I was proud of my accomplishments. I had just celebrated my twentieth anniversary with the company and already I was a vice president. Not everyone can make that claim.

I reached for the phone and called my wife. "Honey, I'm going to be late again. I've got at least a couple more hours of work. Don't hold supper."

"Have you forgotten that tonight is your son's baseball game?" she asked.

"I know, but this work has to be finished before I leave. I'll make it up to him later." I placed the receiver back into its cradle and sat looking at my desk.

"Have you ever thought of tithing?" the gentle voice asked.

"What?"

"Have you ever thought of tithing?" the gentle voice repeated.

"No, I never thought of tithing or much else with all the work I have to do. Who are you? Where are you?"

"I am your guardian angel. I sit here night after night with you and watch you work. I like to watch people work. It must be a lot of fun because I see so many people doing it. How many hours a week do you work?"

"Well, if you are with me, you already know. I work long days and often a good part of my weekends."

"Do you enjoy it?"

"Yes, I do enjoy my work, but it seems the more successful I become, the more work there is to do. I miss having dinner with the family and going to my son's ball games. But there are few people who have accomplished what I have at my age."

"When is the last time you took a vacation with the family?" inquired the angel.

"We took a week to visit my wife's family about three years ago. Can't remember when we took a vacation before that."

"Did you come to this planet looking for a job?" the gentle voice asked with a touch of humor.

"You can't be serious."

"Very serious."

"No. Why would anyone come here to look for a job? I got a job because that's what pays the bills. That's being responsible for my obligations."

"If you did not come to this planet looking for a job, then why did you come?"

"I might ask you the same thing. Why did *you* come here? If you are an angel, why would you *want* to come here?"

"Angels can do anything they want. We can be anything we want. And that makes you very special, because I want to be with you."

"You're kidding! Why would you want to be with me?"

"Because you and I are old friends. We have known each other since the beginning of creation. We made an agreement before you came to this planet — that I would be with you throughout your lifetime to assist and offer guidance when you asked, and only when you asked. So once again I ask, why are you here?"

"I'm here to have a good time. That's what I truly want."

"If I understand you correctly, then work is only a means to an end; it is not the end. Be honest. Are you having a good time?"

"Not really. I don't seem to have much time for that any-more."

"Have you thought about tithing?"

"That's the third time you have brought that up. No, I never think about tithing . . . I'm not even sure what it means. Why do you ask?"

"Because it is what you have called out for."

"I don't recall asking anything about tithing."

"That is true. However, do you recall this evening what thoughts went through your mind when you completed the phone call with your wife?"

"Very clearly. As I hung up the phone and stared at all the paperwork on my desk, I thought, Wouldn't it be nice if I could find a way to go to the ball game. What has that got to do with tithing?"

"Throughout time, many have received messages. These messages were interpreted according to the level of consciousness in which they were received. As conscious awareness grows, however, it is wise to look at old beliefs and reinterpret them from a broader perspective, letting go of what you had once considered the truth to embrace it with a greater understanding.

"Tithing is a concept that has existed throughout the ages. The dictionary says that tithing is a tenth part. As you broaden your perspectives, it is time to give new meaning to this concept. Tithing is related to manifestation. It is said, 'That which you give to God, so shall you receive and tenfold or more.' If you are a divine expression of the Creator, may I suggest that it is time to remember the concept of tithing in relation to the God within?

"How much time and money have you spent in your life expanding your awareness of the God within? Consider the possibilities of tithing 10 percent of your time each day to acknowledge your divine nature and celebrate the essence of life,

"What about setting aside 10 percent of your income to expand your awareness and awaken your potential on all levels of your being physically, emotionally and spiritually and to gift yourself with those things that celebrate the joy of life?"

"But how do you do that?" I asked.

"My I suggest a tithing worksheet?"

"Of course. Share your ideas with me and I will put them on my computer."

Tithing Worksheet

I have 24 hours in a day. I will tithe _____ hours daily _____ weekly _____ monthly to remember and enjoy my real reason for being here.

_____ Having fun with friends and family.

_____ Finding personal time to do the things I love.

_____ Creatively expressing the divine nature of my being.

_____ Meditating on the love within myself and in the world.

_____ Seeing and acknowledging the divine essence in all things.

_____ Expanding my conscious awareness and understanding through meditating, reading, workshops.

_____ Taking time to communicate with my angels.

_____ Attending lectures, seminars, workshops, concerts.

_____ Beginning a journal:

  a. Thoughts, revelations, inspirations and conversations.

  b. Listing *coincidences.*

I make $_____ monthly (yearly). I will tithe a minimum of _____%, which equals $_____ to expand my awareness of myself and my world and awaken the potential within.

Workshops & special events I would like to attend:

_____

_____

_____

_____

Gifts to myself: To enjoy the moment; to bring me peace, joy and harmony physically and emotionally (example: weekly massages; books; music; essences; aromatherapy; art; some thing personal just for me).

_____

_____

_____

_____

I will make time just for me and my family and friends; vacations; special events I desire to attend.

_____

_____

_____

_____

✧ ✧ ✧ ✧

I picked up the stack of papers from my desk and put them into my briefcase and left my office. As I walked down the hallway, I noticed Joe, our production manager, sitting at his desk in front of an impressive pile of papers. As I passed his office, I called out, "Joe, have you ever thought of tithing?"

"What?"

"I said, have you ever thought of tithing?"

"No! What's that?"

"I'll stop by and tell you about it tomorrow. Right now I have to go and watch a ball game."

Do you love yourself enough
to honor yourself?

Divine Order

As I walked out of the office building, I noticed a leather-jacketed young man straddle his motorcycle. In one swift motion his foot came down on the starter pedal and the engine roared. His hand turned the throttle and the engine responded. Raising the kickstand, he placed the bike in gear and quickly accelerated into the street. At the same time, a hundred feet in front of him, an automobile suddenly pulled away from the curb, directly in the young man's path. Its driver was totally unaware of the speeding motorcycle bearing down on him from behind. I gasped as I saw the drama unfold. The young man, unable to stop, swerved to cut between the automobile ahead and another automobile coming toward him in the other lane. The big bike careened off the sides of the automobiles and both the machine and the man spun unceremoniously across the pavement for some distance before coming to a rest against a parked automobile.

I raced down the street to see if I could be of assistance to the injured man. By the time I arrived, several people had gathered. The man was lying on his back, eyes glazed in shock, staring into nowhere. His left leg had been severely injured, leaving a large open wound. What had this young man done to deserve this? I thought.

A gentle voice whispered in my ear, *Everything is in divine order.*

I recognized the voice. It was that of my master teacher.

For the next few weeks those words preoccupied my thoughts. *Everything is in divine order.* I reflected back over time, remembering all the occasions when I had heard others comment, "Everything is is divine order." It was a statement used to justify whatever was happening in the moment. Something seemed incomplete. I wanted more clarity to these words.

"What is it that you desire to know?" the gentle voice asked.

"I understand that everything is in divine order, but it seems that often it is an excuse to justify what has happened in the moment, to absolve everyone from any action they were involved with. In other words, that Divine Plan is predestined and nothing we do will change its course."

"Yes," replied the gentle voice, "you are beginning to unfold one of the great mysteries of your universe. I ask you, is not everything in the universe electromagnetic energy?"

"Yes, it is the foundation of our science. Everything in creation is nothing more than electromagnetic energy. We tend to perceive some things as matter in solid form, but that is only a perception. In reality, it is only energy manifested in a dense form."

"Think for a moment," said the gentle voice. "Focus your mind and call forth another thought form you have often used, one that will bring more clarity to your subject. Call it forth and it will come to you."

I closed my eyes. In my mind's eye I could see the words form before me. *For every action there is an equal and opposite reaction.*

"Very good. Your intuition is serving you well. It is a universal truth. For every action there is an equal and opposite reaction. It is a fundamental truth on which your science is based."

"Yes, of course," I said. "One of my best friends is always saying, 'For every action there is an equal and opposite reaction.' I will never forget it."

"Now take one more step in this journey for your truth. Name one thing in all creation that is not divine."

What a profound question. My mind went blank. Name one thing in all creation that is not divine. "But *all* things are divine," I said, "everything! Everything is a divine expression of the Creator. Everything is divine love expressed. In answer to your question, there is nothing in all creation that is not divine."

"Yes. If everything in creation is divine, then would you agree that everything is always in divine order?"

"Yes, of course," I said. "At no time is anything *not* in divine order."

"Look closely at what you have acknowledged."

Everything in the universe is electromagnetic energy.
For every action there is an equal and opposite reaction.
Everything is in divine order.

"Divine order is the result of your actions, or in some cases, lack of action. Thought sets energy into motion. Your actions create your experiences. Your lack of action allows the action of others to prevail. The young man on the motorcycle could pass off the event by saying, 'Everything is in divine order' and he would be correct. Yet had he taken the time to be more cautious, pull into the street responsibly according to traffic conditions, he would have avoided the accident and still been correct in stating,

'Everything is in divine order.'

"You are correct when you say that some people use this term to justify their experiences, not accepting responsibility for their actions or lack of action, delegating that responsibility to someone or something outside them, assuming it was predestined and that no action on their part would have changed the result. There is no force outside of your own that manifests your reality in the moment. To make a choice is to put energy into motion. Not making a choice is also a choice. You are divine love expressed. How do you choose to express it? This is the answer to the great mystery that many have searched for throughout time."

Everything is in divine order.

I Stand in Awe

It was 1951. The sun was bright and the ground was beginning to dry following the monsoons in Korea. Another soldier accompanied me as we negotiated the mountain trail, each carrying forty pounds of equipment to complete our mission this day. I remember the first time I climbed in Korea. For all the physical training I'd had, I found that my legs were unprepared for mountain climbing, but within a short period of time I was climbing with ease. I was in better-than-average physical condition.

It was midmorning before we took our first break along the trail. Sipping from my canteen, I looked up to see a middle aged Korean man coming down the trail with an A-frame on his back. On the A-frame was a freshly cut log fifteen feet long the diameter of a telephone pole. I watched in awe as the short, 125-pound man nimbly squatted and slipped out from beneath the A-frame, propped it in an upright position with his walking stick and asked if we had a cigarette to share with him.

I knew the country. There were no trees that size within twenty miles. Where had he gotten it, and where was he taking it? What an incredible physical specimen, I thought. Here is a man, no larger than a young boy by my terms, carrying a freshly cut log with ease across a mountain trail, a log that was so heavy that both my companion and I together would be unable to lift it off the ground. Yet this man who existed on a diet mostly of rice was performing a task unlike anyone else I knew. Having finished his cigarette, the man smiled, bowed, thanking us for our gift, slipped under the A-frame and with renewed energy, double-timed down the trail.

As we continued our journey that day I thought, What a magnificent creation the human body is — I have yet to explore its full potential.

The Korean tour was over — for me at least. I was on a troop ship headed home. I felt my body relax fully for the first time in over eighteen months. Orders were given for all troops to be on deck in preparation for our scheduled landing in San Francisco. As the ship approached the Golden Gate bridge, I could only stand with my mouth agape as I looked up at this beautiful structure that spanned the water. I felt so small; even the ship seemed small compared to this incredible testimony to man's ability to create. "It is the most beautiful thing I have ever seen," I whispered as tears filled my eyes. After more than one and a half years of seeing nothing more than a one-story earthen building, I had forgotten what existed in other parts of the world. I wondered if my 125-pound Korean friend would ever see my world.

Since those days, I have taken time to allow myself to be in awe of the world around me, the magnificent buildings and architecture that man has created. I look at the skyscrapers and imagine the awesome pressure that must be exerted on the base of the building and the engineers who had to calculate this on paper before the foundation could be laid. I stand in awe of the shipbuilders who have designed and assembled supertankers, aircraft carriers and cruise ships that contain all the life-support systems for those aboard and become cities in themselves.

I stand in awe of man's accomplishments in his quest to fly. In one century, with humble beginnings, moving quickly to supersonic aircraft and rockets that propel man and instruments to other planets.

I stand in awe of man's ability to perform microscopic and laser surgery, to reconnect severed limbs, to give the gift of eyesight with cataract surgery.

I stand in awe of craftsmen and their beautiful creations in stone, wood, jewelry, painting, music, clothing and other art forms.

I honor those who supply food for humanity. The networking of farmers, grocers and the transportation systems that deliver our needs. Those who design and build automobiles that we enjoy and that provide transportation for our needs.

I stand in awe of the outstanding feats that mankind has accomplished with the human body in sports and other physical challenges. I honor the physically and mentally challenged for their accomplishments to master their world.

I stand in awe of the ever-changing world around me as I watch the shift in consciousness taking place upon the Earth. To see beings take responsibility for their actions, their health, their universe. To see mankind release codependent relationships of limitation and embrace cocreative relationships of joy, peace and harmony, where only the Divine expression of Creative Love moves within it.

I stand in awe . . .
for these are exciting times upon the planet Earth.

Have You Noticed?

Have you noticed
that the seasons were more beautiful this year,
that the colors are brighter,
the sky more blue?
Have you noticed the changes within yourself?
Have you noticed how you grow with each passing day,
with each passing life experience?
No, not grown older but grown wiser,
having more depth to your Being,
more radiant, more beautiful in spirit.

Have you noticed the perfection in all things,
in nature, in your friends and acquaintances, in yourself,
in the grand Earth stage that you stand on,
in Mother Earth herself,
who has supported and nurtured us?

Have you noticed that time seems to be moving faster,
never enough time to accomplish
all that you had planned,
that by the time you have thought of it
there is no time to express it?
There seems to be no past, no future, only Now,
in the moment.

Time is becoming no-time.
We are living in the moment.
Science knows that time exists only in the minds of man,
who created the concept of time
to satisfy their mortal minds.
But the Universe, the Soul
already know that there is no time,
that we live only in the moment.

Have you noticed
that so many seem to wait for an opportunity
to find "time"
to acknowledge Love
for those who have blessed their journey,
those who have brought Warmth to their hearts
and Joy to their lives?
It has occurred to me that there is no time
better than now — in the moment —
to thank all those who have blessed my life.

Love and blessings,
Rich Work

Ordering Information

More information is available on the ideas brought forth in

God this is a good book!

_____ *Awaken to the Healer Within* $16.50
      by Rich Work with Ann Marie Groth
_____ *God this is a good book!* $16.50
      by Rich Work

(3 or more books less 10%)
Please include $3.00 s&h for one book,
$1.00 per additional book.

_____ **Workshop & lecture schedule**

_____ **Information on Harmonic Vibrational Essences**

God this is a good book! and *Awaken to the Healer Within*
are available from your local bookstores.

Name _____

Address _____

City _____ State _____ Zip _____

Date _____ Phone (   ) _____

Send check or money order to:

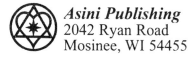 **Asini Publishing**
2042 Ryan Road
Mosinee, WI 54455

Phone and credit card orders: (715) 355-8515
Fax orders: Include credit card information Fax (715) 355-7373

Visit our Web site:
http://www.harmonicsinternational.com/